CAMBRIDGE LIBRARY COLLECTION

Books of enduring scholarly value

Archaeology

The discovery of material remains from the recent or the ancient past has always been a source of fascination, but the development of archaeology as an academic discipline which interpreted such finds is relatively recent. It was the work of Winckelmann at Pompeii in the 1760s which first revealed the potential of systematic excavation to scholars and the wider public. Pioneering figures of the nineteenth century such as Schliemann, Layard and Petrie transformed archaeology from a search for ancient artifacts, by means as crude as using gunpowder to break into a tomb, to a science which drew from a wide range of disciplines - ancient languages and literature, geology, chemistry, social history - to increase our understanding of human life and society in the remote past.

Stonehenge, and Tumuli Wiltunenses

Begun in 1874 and published in 1880, a detailed survey of the stones of Stonehenge was one of the earliest works of William Matthew Flinders Petrie (1853–1942), the energetic archaeologist who is remembered as a pioneering Egyptologist. It is reissued here alongside Sir Richard Colt Hoare's 1829 analysis of the barrows surrounding Stonehenge, thus giving modern readers a valuable two-part snapshot of nineteenth-century investigations into this famous site. Hoare (1758–1838), a Wiltshire baronet with a keen interest in archaeology and topography, conducted excavations on the site of the stones in the early 1800s, which were later referred to by Petrie, whose measurements were much more accurate (up to one tenth of an inch). Petrie's numbering system for the stones, as set out in this publication, is still in use today. Many of his groundbreaking works in Egyptology are also reissued in the Cambridge Library Collection.

Cambridge University Press has long been a pioneer in the reissuing of out-of-print titles from its own backlist, producing digital reprints of books that are still sought after by scholars and students but could not be reprinted economically using traditional technology. The Cambridge Library Collection extends this activity to a wider range of books which are still of importance to researchers and professionals, either for the source material they contain, or as landmarks in the history of their academic discipline.

Drawing from the world-renowned collections in the Cambridge University Library and other partner libraries, and guided by the advice of experts in each subject area, Cambridge University Press is using state-of-the-art scanning machines in its own Printing House to capture the content of each book selected for inclusion. The files are processed to give a consistently clear, crisp image, and the books finished to the high quality standard for which the Press is recognised around the world. The latest print-on-demand technology ensures that the books will remain available indefinitely, and that orders for single or multiple copies can quickly be supplied.

The Cambridge Library Collection brings back to life books of enduring scholarly value (including out-of-copyright works originally issued by other publishers) across a wide range of disciplines in the humanities and social sciences and in science and technology.

Stonehenge,
and
Tumuli Wiltunenses

W.M. Flinders Petrie
Richard Colt Hoare

 CAMBRIDGE
UNIVERSITY PRESS

CAMBRIDGE
UNIVERSITY PRESS

University Printing House, Cambridge, CB2 8BS, United Kingdom

Cambridge University Press is part of the University of Cambridge.

It furthers the University's mission by disseminating knowledge in the pursuit of
education, learning and research at the highest international levels of excellence.

www.cambridge.org
Information on this title: www.cambridge.org/9781108076852

© in this compilation Cambridge University Press 2015

This edition first published 1829–80
This digitally printed version 2015

ISBN 978-1-108-07685-2 Paperback

This book reproduces the text of the original edition. The content and language reflect
the beliefs, practices and terminology of their time, and have not been updated.

Cambridge University Press wishes to make clear that the book, unless originally published
by Cambridge, is not being republished by, in association or collaboration with,
or with the endorsement or approval of, the original publisher or its successors in title.

The original edition of this book contains a number of oversize plates
which it has not been possible to reproduce to scale in this edition.
They can be found online at www.cambridge.org/9781108076852

STONEHENGE:

PLANS, DESCRIPTION, AND THEORIES.

BY

W. M. FLINDERS PETRIE,

AUTHOR OF 'INDUCTIVE METROLOGY,' &c.

LONDON:

EDWARD STANFORD, 55 CHARING CROSS, S.W.

1880.

INTRODUCTION.

THE lack of any thoroughly accurate survey of Stonehenge will be a sufficient reason for the production of the present plan, in addition to those already published. Neither the plans of Wood, Smith, Colt Hoare, Sir Henry James, nor Hawkshaw, lay any claim apparently to accuracy greater than a few inches, thus missing important results and deductions; whereas that now produced is correct to a few tenths of an inch, in fact quite as closely as the surface of the stone can be estimated in most cases.

Though on a small scale for convenience of use, the accuracy of this plan is as great as that of a sheet of ordinary delicacy about 4 or 5 feet across. The original measurements of the stone circle, on the triangulation lines, and the well-wrought stones, were taken to the nearest $\frac{1}{10}$ of an inch, and in all cases correct to within $\frac{1}{4}$ inch; the plotting and copying (on double the scale now lithographed) were correspondingly done to about a thousandth of an inch, in many parts with a magnifier: the present photolithograph is therefore intentionally accurate to $\frac{1}{2000}$ of an inch; and, considering the various sources of error, it may be usefully examined, and measurements taken from it, to $\frac{1}{500}$ or $\frac{1}{1000}$ of an inch. Those readers who merely wish for approximate ideas, can use this for general inspection like any rougher plan; but for investigations on the arrangement and exact dimensions of any part, this plan, measured with an accurate plotting scale and magnifier, will probably give results as trustworthy as could be obtained on the ground.

The work was begun in 1874, but after going some way with it, it was abandoned owing to the errors of the ordinary surveying chain used. In 1877 I made a new pattern of chain, expressly for accurate work;* and with this the present survey was made, in June and September of that year. It was laid by, partly owing to being engaged with plans of the other remains in the southern counties, and partly waiting to obtain accurate sunrise observations at midsummer.

* The essentials of this pattern are, 1st, rhomboidal eyes; 2nd, long links of 20 inches; 3rd, no intermediate rings; 4th, dividing marks on the middles of the links, fixed (from the official standard) after the chain is made and strained; 5th, numbering marks on every link; 6th, lightness, for stretching without perceptible error over hollows.

The theoretical considerations of the date and origin of this structure are necessarily entered on here, as many of the details now brought to light bear strongly on those questions; but the object of this publication is more to state facts than theories.

In order to give a fair impression, all the considerations of importance have been mentioned, on each side of the argument, that could be found by careful reading and personal reference; and as my own opinion has fluctuated more than once, I may at least hope to have attained thorough impartiality.

The various sections are divided as follows :—

FACTS.

1. Description of the Plans.
2. Details of the Stones.
3. Methods of Workmanship.
4. Number of Stones.

THEORIES.

5. The Work not complete.
6. Position of the "Altar Stone."
7. Midsummer Sunrise.
8. Sequence shown by Construction.
9. Sequence shown by Measures.
10. Objects Found.
11. Summary of Evidences on Pre-Roman Age.
12. Summary of Evidences on Post-Roman Age.
13. Summary of Evidences on the Use.
14. Concluding Remarks.

STONEHENGE.

1. Description of the Plans.

BESIDE the explanation given on the plans, some general arrangements require notice, before mentioning the stones in detail. Offsets were taken to fix the various points, but their estimated rectangularity was never trusted beyond a few inches, all long lines being tied in by triangulation. The arrows projecting from the stones, show the extent to which the top of each stone has shifted by leaning; this was estimated by considering both faces of the stones, but owing to their often tapering, the extremity of the arrow does not necessarily show the place of the top of the face. It may be reckoned that the ground-level outline of the stone, shown on the plan, has moved about $\frac{1}{10}$ of the shift of the top. The thinner outline of the form above the ground, is only given when the stone is more regular above than below; as its position was arranged probably with reference to its most regular part. The more regular part is always the most prominent (except on the back of No. 52), as the stone was shaped at its largest part. The character of the shading, &c., is sufficiently explained on the plan. The five stones "standing in 1747" are from Wood's plan; and as they are overthrown, or much shifted since his time, it seemed desirable to make this plan as complete as possible by inserting them. They were plotted from Wood's measurements, in connection with neighbouring stones still unshifted, and then adjusted by means of the latter on this plan. Of course their positions and their outlines are far less accurate than those of the other stones, but they are nevertheless the best now to be had; and their present positions are also shown in unshaded dotted outline. No distinction is made on this plan between perfect stones and mere stumps of which the upper part is removed (though these are detailed in the description), as for considerations of arrangement this is wholly immaterial—unlike the shift, which is important.

The large circle is the mean circle which agrees best to all the sarsen stones,[*] making

* These are tertiary sandstones left lying on the chalk after the denudation of those beds. The bluestones are from Cornwall or Ireland.

allowance for their shiftings. The next circle similarly is fitted to the outer bluestones ; though to what point of them it should agree is not certain, as their inner faces are often convex, unlike the sarsens ; whether the innermost curve, or the inner corners of the stone, or something between, is not clear. The trilithons* are not on a circle, and the scheme of their placing is obscure. The innermost semicircle is fitted to the bluestones, like the others. The centres of these three circles, and of the outer earth circle, are shown surrounded by little rings on the plan ; the radii of these little rings are equal in each case to the mean error of the various points of the respective circles from a true figure. This mean error of the inner bluestones is $1\cdot7$ inch ; of the outer bluestones, 8 inches ; of the sarsen circle, $3\cdot2$ inches ; and of the earth circle (shown in Plate II.), 10 inches. The two fine lines crossing obliquely near the centre, will be seen to be in line with four short pieces on the outskirts of the plan, numbered 91, 92, 93, and 94. These are the lines connecting the centres of the stones (91 and 93), and of the pits or barrows (92 and 94), shown in Plate II., lying on the outer earth circle. They so nearly intersect the centre, that it is important to show them on this delicate plan ; their probable error is about $\pm$ 2 inches $= \frac{1}{100}$ inch on the plan.

The mean axis was determined by (1) the middle of the entrance, which is closely the same at all heights of the stones, though the opening widens 20 inches at the top ; (2) the centre of the main circle ; (3) the estimated original place of the great trilithon stones 55 and 56, considering that they have slewed northwards in falling ; the estimated distance between them, eliminating the slew, is 13 inches, and this (though quite independent) closely agrees with the standing trilithons which are $12\cdot8$ and $12\cdot4$ inches ; (4) half the average spacing between the stones, allowed from the side of No. 16 ; this is very vague, as the interval varies from 26 to 51 inches ; the mean, being 36, gives 18 for the half-distance.

The mean axis drawn differs from these elements as follows :—

Axis.

Exactly through	entrance opening.
	$\cdot6$ inch from sarsen circle centre.
From estimated centre of trilithon, $\cdot4$ inch	
Approximately by No. 16, $1\cdot8$,,	

---

* This term is here restricted to the five internal groups, of two uprights and one impost each, and not applied to the circle stones, as by some writers.

The very close agreement of the elements is remarkable, but each was determined before they were compared.

Qutside the circle will be seen five crosses on each side of the plan, beside others in the circle; these are exactly 25 feet or 300 inches apart; they may be considered the corners of squares of 25 feet (or a large square of 100 feet quartered in each direction), drawn on the mean axis as a basis, the sides being omitted to avoid confusion. The object is to give a scale extending over every part of the plan, so that distortion in photolithographing, and irregular contraction of the paper, may be eliminated for accurate measurements; a scale drawn at the edge in the usual way, is peculiarly liable to derangement; and for rough purposes any inch measure will do, as the plan is on the simple scale of $\frac{1}{200}$.

It should be remembered in comparing this plan with others, or with accurate measurements, that some inches difference may easily occur if the stones be not measured on the same level as here; in all cases the most perfect part of the stone was taken close to the ground, and if it had a better form above, this is also shown.

To Wood's plan (1747), Smith (in 1770) added Nos. 39, 72, and 160 a; Colt Hoare adds No. 71; Hawkshaw adds a piece which I could not see, between 14 and 36; and finally I may add 66, which makes its first appearance in this plan.

The second plan is not of such accuracy as the first; the stones are only approximately reduced, within about $\frac{1}{500}$ inch; and the earth circle may perhaps in parts have some errors as large. Its mean error already stated (10 inches) was determined by a large scale plan. A true circle is here drawn, with short breaks at each measured point, such points being shown by a small cross, more or less in or out of the true line; thus enabling the differences to be easily seen. The distance of the outer ditch and bank was measured in four places, also marked on the plan. The levels of them, taking the area levels as o, are thus :—

Top of bank .. .. + 9 to 18 variation, + 14 mean

= rise 41 } from bottom

Bottom of ditch .. − 16 to 39 „ − 27 „

= rise 17 } of ditch.

Top of faint outer bank − 16 to + 1 „ − 10 „

The levels of the various parts of the area are marked in inches and tenths, above the Ordnance bench-mark on the Friar's Heel, No. 96.

The method of marking banks and ditches, &c., has been adopted, after much consideration and experiment, as being free from the ambiguity of ordinary shading, and also admitting of greater precision of drawing.

The two mounds within the area are shown on this plan; they have been often called pits (from Wood), owing to their having a hole in the top, probably from old diggings in them. The northern one is nearly half cut away by a road; it has a ditch and bank, unlike the other. The forms of all the outlying stones, Nos. 91, 93, 95, and 96, are given in the corner of Plate I.; the closer shade on 91 showing approximately the place of the base, before it tipped outward.

The details of the junction of the circle and the avenue, and of the banks that cross the avenue lower down, are all carefully entered, exactly as they appear on the ground.

The avenue is raised between the banks, which are very faint on their inner edges, and in all parts flat and ill-defined. The north-east end and the branches are very faint, and scarcely traceable in parts. The greater width of the north branch is curious, and as it is not noticed in the small plans of the Ordnance Survey and Hoare, there would almost seem to be some uncertainty in the plan, as it has not been verified; three measured points on each side however agree.

The parallel banks are quite unnoticed in Hoare's and the Ordnance plans. They are slight but sharp, and the ground between them has been lowered. Of what date they may be is not certain, but if not intended for a recent road they are probably ancient. Against the idea of a road there are the following facts: (1) They are 42 feet apart, but the road they would join is the usual regulation width of 30 feet; (2) there is no ditch, and the ground is flat between; whereas the main requisite of a road is to raise the centre, and make side ditches; (3) they end abruptly, and have been recommenced farther easterly (traceable by lines of buttercups, though now ploughed), and also westerly as seen on the small plan of $\frac{1}{10000}$ on Plate II.; this discontinuous work is not like modern road making; (4) the western part passes a barrow; and here, instead of cutting a slice out of it to make room for a road, the bank runs up over the foot of the barrow, and the barrow ditch is flattened at its edges but not filled up; also the barrow is just in the midst of the length of this piece. All these points are unlike the beginning of a modern road. The banks pass over the avenue west bank and ditch, but are cut away at the east bank sharply, to allow of a cart track passing, which runs down the avenue bank. This looks as if they were older than the cart track, and therefore not recent.

The row of barrows on the $\frac{1}{10000}$ plan are very nearly in a straight line, except the last. Their average departure of their centres is 52 inches, on a line 850 feet long in all. Further details of their distances are given in 9. *Sequence shown by Measures.*

---

2. Details of the Stones.

After much consideration, the irregular lettering and numbering of Colt Hoare was abandoned; it begins with the entrance stones as A^1 and A^2, goes then to the trilithons B^1 B^2 . . . F^1 F^2, thus not leaving enough letters for the outer circle without a double alphabet, and then using numbers for the bluestones. The present system is entirely by numbers for each stone; lettering the fragments of a single stone, as 59 a, 59 b, 59 c. The order begins always at the axis, and goes with positive rotation E., S., W., N. 1 to 30 are the outer sarsens (allowing numbers for the blank spaces); 31 to 49 the outer bluestones; 51 to 60 the trilithons; 61 to 72 the inner bluestones; 80 the "altar stone"; 91 to 96 the outlying stones and tumuli; the lintels are all numbered 100 more than their higher numbered supporter; i. e. the numbers agreeing with 1 prefixed to the lintel. Thus the numbering of the sarsens begins at 1 and 51, and the bluestones at 31 and 61; an easily remembered arrangement. The numbers of the successive circles are all in sequence, though each set begins a fresh decade; except that No. 50 is unapplied, but as a lintel in that set has no supporter it appropriates No. 150 very suitably.

The following details of the stones are accompanied by Hoare's lettering for reference. The levels are in inches above the Ordnance bench-mark on the Friar's Heel, No. 96. The heights are above the ground at the spot in question. The word "Outline" is reserved for fallen stones; "Plan" for the horizontal section of stones. "Emergence" is the line of the face at ground-level. "Impost" is used for a trilithon top-stone; "Lintel" for a circle top-stone.

No.	Hoare.	Height.	Level of top.	Diff. from mean of group (213·3).	REMARKS.
Sarsens.					
1	A^1	159	208·1	− 5·2	
2		170	211·9	− 1·4	
3		171	209·3	− 4·0	
4		170	211·9	− 1·4	

C

No. Sarsens.	Hoare.	Height.	Level of top.	Diff. from mean of group (213·3).	REMARKS.
5		174	215·0	+ 1·7	
6		165	215·9	+ 2·6	
7		162	211·3	− 2·0	
8		..	..	..	Sides worked.
9 a, b		..	..	..	9 b, sides worked; end very flat, with tenon.
10		160	220·0	+ 6·7	
11		96	..	..	
12		..	..	..	Two tenons on end.
14*		..	..	..	31 to 36 thick.
15		..	..	..	Two tenons on end.
16		165	215·5	+ 2·2	Bench-mark at 78·3 level.
19		..	..	..	End and north side worked. Top 13 out of ground.
21		152	212·7	− ·6	
22		153	209·2	− 4·1	
23		153	209·4	− 3·9	
25		..	..	..	Fallen westwards.
26		..	..	..	No worked faces.
27		167	214·2	+ ·9	
28		165	214·4	+ 1·1	
29		156	212·3	− 1·0	
30	A²	153	207·6	− 5·7	
Bluestones.					
31	1	..	127·5	..	Rounded top, broken.
32	3	..	..	..	Foot buried, fixed by probing; two faces shown here on top. 17·5 thick, all down.
33	4	..	..	..	
34	5	38	..	..	Upright.
35 a, b	6, n n		..	..	Only a stump, widely cracked, like two stones. 35 b, probably part of 35 a.
36	7	..	..	..	North end buried; a square stone lying with edge up, emerging at lines drawn across face.
37	8	..	..	..	} Schistose, see 14, shaded plans from Wood, 1747.
39	10	..	..	..	
40	11	..	..	..	Overthrown before 1747.

* 14 was leaning on 38 in 1747 emerging at the full line; it now has fallen farther, occupying the dotted outline, and resting on 38, at a slope of 1 in 4. 38 has apparently tipped over sideways, as well as inwards, owing to the pressure of 14 upon its east corner; having been in 1747 in the shaded plan, and now emerging at the dotted line (which also shows place of east end under turf), rising 45° to north. 39 occupied the shaded plan on end in 1747, but has been pushed inwards to the present dotted outline by the fall of 14, and now rises 1 in 2 to north.

No.	Hoare.	Height.	Level of top.	Diff. from mean of group.	REMARKS.
Bluestones.					
41	12	..	..	..	No flat faces. Small cross at estimated original site of centre.
42	13	..	..	..	Fallen in 1747, before trilithon fell.
43	14	..	..	..	On edge. Rises 50° to east.
44	15	..	..	..	Small cross as above, but shifted altogether (?).
45	16	..	..	..	„ „ „ . Flat sides and top.
46	17	..	..	..	Hornstone.
47	18	..	..	..	Leaning in, outline of top shown.
48	19	..	..	..	Hornstone as 46.
49	20	..	132·9	..	Broken, rounded at top.
Sarsens.					
51	B¹	201	252·4	..	
52	B²	..	255·7	..	
53	C¹	212	265·2	..	
54	C²				
55 a, b, D¹		..	..	..	At south end a large projecting foot left in working, to go under ground. Concave on inner face.
56	D²	..	..	..	The leaning stone. The shaded part south of it shows how far back (at the least) it must have been when upright. This trilithon upset by the Duke of Buckingham digging in 1620.
57	E¹	..	..	..	This trilithon fell 3rd January, 1797. Shaded plans from Wood, 1747.
58	E²	..	..	..	Dotted outlines show the present places.
59 a,b,c F¹		..	..	..	Fallen before 1575 ; see view in Camden.
60	F²	198	247·8	..	
Bluestones.			Mean 148·8.		
61	21	..	125·0	..	Broken top.
62	22	..	143·0	− 5·8	
63	23	..	147·0	− 1·8	
64	24	..	..	..	Only a stump, 3 inches high.
65	25	..	..	..	Broken near ground.
66 omitted		..	..	..	Only a stump.
67	27	..	..	..	Larger stone, different in style to others.
68	26	..	153·1	+ 4·3	Worked groove down north side. Supports 56.
69	28	..	157·0	+ 8·2	
70	29	..	144·1	− 4·7	Tipped out by foot of 58 in falling. Shaded plan Wood's, dotted outline present place. Wood is wrong in shape.
71	30	..	..	..	
72	31	..	..	..	

No. Bluestones.	Hoare.	Height.	Level of top.	Diff. from mean of group.	REMARKS.
80 Altar stone	..	mid	60·0	..	Rises east, at a slope = 7·3 on whole length.
91	..	..	..	..	This leans outward; the outline is shown in Plate II. No working.
92	..	..	..	..	Mound with central pit.
93	..	..	..	..	Upright stone. A patch on each side, and on outer face, wrought.
94	..	..	..	..	Mound with central pit, ditch and ridge around. Half cut away by road.
95	..	..	..	..	Lying quite flat, upper face at ground level. Wrought end and sides.
96 Friar's heel	..		..	..	Leaning west, unwrought.
101	..	..	top 237·6	..	Across entrance.
102	..	..	237·3	..	Lintels *in situ.* Not shown on ground plan.
105	..	..	241·6	..	
107	..	..	239·9	..	
120	..	..	..	..	Portion of lintel, top 16 inches out of ground.
122	..	..	239·5	..	*In situ*, not on ground plan.
127	..	..	..	..	Sides worked, ends broken.
130	..	..	240·5	..	*In situ*, not on plan.
150	..	..	..	..	Bluestone impost, unsuited for any existing pair.
152	..	{mid un-derside}	252·7	..	252·2 at north end. *In situ,* not on plan.
154	..	„	265·2	..	
156	D³	..	..	..	Lintel overthrown 1620. Marks on it cut in 1827 or 8.
158	E³	..	..	..	Lintel fell in 1797.
160 a,b,c F³		..	..	..	Fragments of lintel. No trace of mortises on upper sides.

The original height of the fallen trilithons 55–58 out of the ground was carefully estimated; all together they are as follows :—

		inches.		inches.	
Nos.	51, 52	201, top of upright;		241, top of impost.	
	53, 54	212	„	256	„
	55, 56	263 ± 2	„	288 ± 2	„
	57, 58	214 ± 3	„	258?	„
	59, 60	198	„	238?	„

The dimensions of the imposts, and trilithon tops, &c., vary so irregularly that they do not seem worth detailing. The average dimensions are, with the mean of the differences from the average,

	inches.			inches.		
Trilithon tops ..	73·2 long,	2·5	mean difference;	39·7 wide,	3·9	mean difference.
Imposts	184·2 „	2·6	„	48·0 (at ends)	2·7	„
Circle stones tops..	67·1 „	5·0	„	31·5	6·0	„
Lintels	133·7 „	2·8	„	41·0	3·0	„
Tenons apart ..	34·3	5·0	„			

The ground levels are marked on Plate II., like the preceding, in inches above the bench-mark on the Heel stone, 96.

The circle of the tops of the sarsens has apparently a tilt, according to the levels, averaging at the maximum 4 inches above and below the mean level; the nodes of the plane being at No. 5, and opposite, and the highest point between 27 and 28. The assumption of this tilt reduces the mean error from a true plane, from 2·75 to 1·9 inches (or as 10:7); it is most likely that they would not be placed in exactly a level plane, and the tilt of 4 inches = 24'. The mean level of the circle tops, 213·3 above datum, is not the mean of existing stones (212·4), as their irregular distribution would affect it; but it is the mean of the 4 mean levels of the 4 quadrants.

Whether the stones were arranged by their inner or outer faces, is settled by the fact that the inner faces fit a mean circle, with just half the amount of error of the outer faces: observe Nos. 1, 2, 3, and 21, 22, and 23. Also the flattest sides are placed in, very plainly seen on the ground in 3, 28, 29, and specially 2 and 60. 52 and 54, though better on the back above, have the best side of the base placed inwards.

The azimuths of the principal lines are as follows:—

Mean axis of circle as drawn	30' ± 2'
Mean axis of avenue..	18'
Middle of avenue from middle of entrance	15'
Axis symmetrical with 91, 93, 92, 94 ..	0' (adopted as arbitrary datum).

The avenue axis apparently runs to 14 inches north-west of the middle of the entrance; but the banks are so very vague, and so much damaged near the circle, that this is not very certain; perhaps ± 5 inches.*

---

3. Methods of Workmanship.

Nearly all of the stones have had more or less dressing; some dressed all over, others only on prominent parts; so as to give a regular figure at the end or edges, with faulty parts elsewhere. The method of cleaving the stone is shown by the large flat stone 95, one corner of which has been begun to be cut off; a row of 6 holes, 1½ inch long, ¾ wide, 1 and 1¼ deep, and averaging 6 inches apart (varying from 4 to 8), are sunk in nearly a straight

* This sign ± is used throughout to denote "probable error"; i. e. the truth is as likely to be within 5 inches on either side of the statement, as to be over 5 inches from it : *vide* De Morgan, Airy, Merriman &c.

line; they are sloping sided, as would be made by irregular tools. There are no traces of such cleaving holes on the edges of any of the other stones, apparently owing to their subsequent dressing. Large quantities were cut away in surface work; the projecting foot left on 55 shows about 15 inches of stone to have been cut away all across the face of the block. The method of cutting down a face was by running large shallow grooves across the stone, probably cutting away the intervening ridges in making the next series of grooves; these wide grooves were then apparently removed by running narrower ones across them. The wide ones are finely shown on the back of 59, one 17 wide and $2\frac{1}{2}$ deep, with a sharp ridge on either side, and with three faint cross grooves. On the side of 59 next to 60 there are small grooves, 6 in a width of 22 inches, the best of them 48 long, all very flat. No grooving is left on 55, though so much has been cut out. The back of 54 has 3 large vertical grooves, 50, 20, and 28 wide; also slight cross grooves, 4 in a width of 39 inches. On the back of 52 there are two faint horizontal grooves in 11 inches wide; also one slight horizontal ridge left on the flat inner face of 51. The only grooving on the bluestones is on 67; a slight vertical groove 14 wide, and 2 or 3 horizontal ones at 2 or 3 inches apart: this stone is a very dissimilar shape to the others, being wide, flat, and thickest at the top.

The tenons have been worked to an irregular mammiform shape; those fallen are much damaged, and have nearly disappeared in some cases; but the finest for examination is on the top of 60, reached by a ladder, being 17 feet from the ground. Here the general surface is very flat, all carefully picked; and though showing the picking, yet apparently a true plane within the depth of the pickmarks. A ridge runs along the outer, north-west, side, 3 inches high, and a slight ridge on south-west. The tenon is $15\frac{1}{2}$ inches wide at base, and 7 inches high. There is a similar sort of tray shape, with a raised edge $2\frac{1}{2}$ inches high, on the top of 51; the impost (still *in situ*) having a corresponding sinking around its edge to fit the ledge on the edge of the upright. The top of 52 is similarly cut, with a ledge 1 inch high, and dressed very smooth and regular. This is seen as they are not erected with the tops quite parallel, 51 sloping down 1·2 inches to 52, on the 77 inches of its top width, thus leaving a gap.

The trilithon imposts are cut 5 and 6 inches wider at the top than the under side; and are flat on the inner, and convex on the outer side.

Whether the mortise holes were cut to fit the distance of the tenons, after erecting the stones, or whether the work was first planned and the stones erected to fit the mortises, is not clear in the outer circle; probably the latter, as there is a ridge $1\frac{1}{2}$ inch high across the top of 30, rising between the lintel blocks. The lintel 101 has a projecting tongue at the middle of each end, keying into a corresponding vertical groove in the adjacent block; 130 has the corresponding groove on the end joining 101, and a tongue on the other end; the next lintel with corresponding groove is lost. 102 is similar, with a groove for the tongue of 101, and a tongue on the other end. 122 has a tongue on each end, which projects about 3 inches like the others. 130 has a curious mistake in it, of a third mortise hole, too large, and too near its middle.

---

4. Number of Stones.

The decimal numbers of many stone circles is worth notice, in connection with Stonehenge. The outer circle of sarsens has 30 stones (or places); the trilithons are 10 stones; and the bluestones are probably incomplete. Similarly the circle at Winterbourne Abbas, Dorset, has 10 stones (one missing); the circles of Dawnsmaen, Boscawenoon, and Kenidjack, in the Land's End, are each of 20 stones; and though the latter have also some missing, and it might be questioned whether a gap was not left intentionally, yet it does not affect the point that the circle is divided into a decimal number of places, though each may not contain a stone. The trouble of dividing decimally, instead of continued halving into 8, 16, or 32, or taking $\frac{1}{6}$ by the radius, shows that importance was attached to it, especially as it is so frequent. Other cases, where the circle is less perfect, are less decisive; but the three circles of the Hurlers near St. Cleer are credited with having had 29, 29, and 27 stones, which may very possibly have been 30 originally. In Cumberland, the Eskdale circle was of 40 or 41 stones, the Swinside circle of 60 stones, and the Gunnerskeld circle, Westmoreland, 29 + or − 1 stones, or spaces for stones, which show apparently the same decimal division.

---

5. The Work not complete.

Though it is certain that some stones have been removed, this fact does not account for the whole case. First, the evidence for the stones being removed. Inigo Jones says that some bluestones were taken away since he first saw them. The Earl of Pembroke told

Aubrey that an altar stone was found in the middle of the area, and carried away to St. James's *; there is, however, no such stone in Inigo Jones's plan, nor is there any hole or sharp sinking of the earth in the middle of the area, such as would be left by abstracting a large stone sunken in the ground. No stones are missing since Wood's plan in 1747. There are several stones that have been overthrown and broken, and of which only portions remain, see Nos. 8, 15, 19, and 26; from each of these at least half the stone has been removed for certain. Also of four bluestones only stumps remain, Nos. 35, 64, 65, and 66; a further evidence of violence and of removal.

The evidence for non-completion of the outer sarsens, is in the very much smaller stone 11; this is only half the usual breadth, and 8 feet instead of 14 feet high like the others. At the same time, as it exactly occupies the proper place between 10 and 12, and (allowing for its tip out) fits the circle better than some others, we cannot deny the intention of its similarity. Again, Nos. 21 and 23 are both defective in size, compared with the rest; these show that 11 was no single freak, but was the result of not having better material. If then the builders ran so short as to have to use such a stone as 11, is it not very probable that they had not enough to finish the circle? Whether the site of Stonehenge was determined by a quantity of large sarsens occurring there, from the denudation of the beds above, or whether they were collected from far, is uncertain; there are few or none such large sarsens to be found now elsewhere. The absence of any blocks of waste stone, and of any smaller sarsens unsuitable for building, near the site, suggests that the blocks were collected from all parts, and trimmed before carriage; though the fitting of tenons, &c., might be done at the structure. Might any fragments be found at the groups of sarsens elsewhere, showing the remains of the cleavage holes? The chips of bluestone and sarsen together in the barrows, would seem to have been chipped off after erection; as we shall see that there is internal evidence that the bluestones are later than the sarsens.

The outer bluestones have been usually supposed to be the remains of a complete circle; there are at present 18 (perhaps 19); and the places seem to be 44, if they were equally arranged. Now a point apparently hitherto unnoticed in their positions is that 14 out of the 18 are in pairs opposite to one another (31, 34?, 36, and 43, being the only unpaired stones); and also that in the four 37 to 40, and in the four 46 to 49 which match them, there occur two stones in each set which are dissimilar to all the others,

* ? Berwick St. James, near Stonehenge.

being schistose or hornstone in place of syenite. If the circle ever were complete, it is highly improbable that the spoilers would remove stones always in pairs opposite to each other. The probability of 14 out of 18 stones being by chance opposite to each other in a set of 44 places is about 5000 to 1. The stone No. 44 is omitted in this consideration, as its original place is not quite certain; but if in the outer bluestones, it probably paired to 34, which would increase the improbability of casualty to over 30,000 to 1. Thus there is practical proof, from the arrangement, that there never were many more bluestones.

The celebrated bluestone impost 150 is another evidence of incompletion; for if ever erected, and then overthrown, the loose lintel would naturally be removed before the supporters. It will not fit any of the existing bluestones, as the mortises are (judging by the sarsen imposts) too close together for any now standing; and it cannot be intended for one of a set of continuous lintels, as its ends beyond the holes are too long. It is just adapted for a very close pair of bluestones, proportioned like the trilithons. The idea that some of the fallen bluestones may likewise be imposts, lying with the holes downwards, is unlikely when examined in detail; 36 has certainly been an upright, and the fallen ones 41 to 45 are mostly buried more or less at one end, and are all much more irregular than 150, 45 being the only one at all approaching its regularity of cutting. Hence 150 seems to be unique.

The flat stone 95 on the earth circle is another evidence of incompletion, as across one corner a row of holes is sunk for cleaving it (see large outline in corner of Plate I.), which have never been carried out. The sides and ends are trimmed, and the whole is as large as a trilithon upright; but it has no trace of tenons on the end, which is flat, smooth, and good. Its present position is a puzzle; the surface is very irregular on the upper face, which is, however, as nearly level, and also as nearly flush with the ground surface, as it can be estimated. The sides are now exposed, owing evidently to modern digging for examination of it. By its sunken position and absence of any dip it seems unlikely that it was in progress to another site, or that it was to be placed on end where it now lies, or that it has fallen. But it lies askew, in a manner unlike any other stone, except the "altar," No. 80, which makes it not look as if finally fixed. In lying to one side of the axis it resembles No. 96. Were these ever to be paired by others, forming narrow gateways in the avenue?

D

6. Position of the "Altar Stone."

With regard to the altar stone, its skew position, as in No. 95, is against its being now in its intended site; and for and against the theory of its having stood as the impost of a second trilithon, on the top of trilithon 55, 56, we may note : (1) Henry of Huntingdon's well-known description, which Hoare explains as referring to the trilithons seen over the circle lintels; (2) that it lies skew at present; (3) that there are traces of what may be either natural hollows or shallow mortises for supporters on the top of the impost 154, at 18 to $30\frac{1}{2}$ from north end and 26 to 38 from south end; the true mortise holes underneath being at 9 to $28\frac{1}{2}$ from north end, and $24\frac{1}{2}$ to $50\frac{1}{2}$ from south end.   But against the theory, (1) the altar is 198 long, though partly buried, and found by probing at the ends, the impost being only 184 long; and as none of the imposts overhang, it is unlikely that a super-impost would do so; (2) it lies nearly flat at present without more slope (7 inches on 200) than might easily be produced by the Duke of Buckingham's and Cunnington's diggings; (3) it is deeply sunk in the ground, and that regularly, and not on an edge which might dig in in falling; whereas the impost 158 is said in falling only to have struck 7 inches deep, even on its edge; (4) it is unlikely that any person would or could displace it, if perched on the top of a trilithon 24 feet high; any other damage, such as digging down the trilithon altogether, would be easier done; (5) and there are no supporters remaining for it.

---

7. Midsummer Sunrise.

The popular idea of the sun rising on the longest day behind the Friar's Heel, No. 96, was carefully tested by theodolite observations.   When duly corrected for excentricities of theodolite and of signal, for minute change of declination between epochs of solstice and observation, and for altitude of horizon on rising slightly to the back of the circle, the azimuths are

	From middle entrance.	From behind middle trilithon.
Middle of avenue at parallel banks	15'	
True axis of avenue, 18'.		
Axis of circle, 30' ± 2'.		
North side of Friar's Heel	32'	11'
Peak „ „	1° 45'	1° 24'
South side „ „	2° 45'	2° 24'
Beginning of sunrise, midsummer 1880	1° 4'	1° 2'
Middle „ „	1° 30'	1° 28'
End „ „	1° 57'	1° 55'

Now as the azimuth of sunrise varies with the declination, its extreme place at the solstice will of course vary with secular changes of declination, just as its rising at other times of year varies with the diurnal variation ; and as the obliquity of the ecliptic is decreasing, and has been so for all historic time, it follows that the sun at the solstice has risen at a greater azimuth, or more easterly than now ; and will rise at a less azimuth, or more westerly.

Which of the above nine azimuths of the structure is intended to agree with which of the three solar azimuths ? There are thus twenty-seven modes of connection ; further, the three solar azimuths are continuously in motion, and will each in the course of ages agree to each of the nine structural azimuths; beside casual small changes, by fluctuations of horizontal refraction, caused by heat or pressure, easily making 2′ or 3′ change of azimuth of apparent rising.

As the sun's azimuth of rising is decreasing, we may reject all structural azimuths less than that of the beginning of the present rising ; and further, as Stonehenge is certainly over 1000 years old, we may reject all azimuths up to 19′ farther east, i. e. all less than 1° 23′, which was the azimuth of beginning of rising at that time. Thus five azimuths are entirely cut out of consideration ; those of all the axes, and the north side of the Heel stone : and as the north side is certainly of no importance, it cannot be supposed that the south side of the stone (far below the horizon) should be of importance, when it has a remarkably peaked top, which is unlike that of any other stone there, and which gives a definite horizon azimuth. Is, then, the peak to be observed from the middle of the entrance, or from the slit between the middle trilithon ? First, the entrance is 50 inches wide, and its middle is not easily settled without measurement; whereas the slit between the trilithon was only 13 inches wide, about the same as the peak of the Heel stone, the estimated middle of which would give a good definite azimuth on a length of 3400 inches. Next, the horizon is invisible at the entrance, the peak of the Heel rising far above it ; and it is only on retreating up the slight rise, to behind the middle trilithon, that the horizon is seen on the level of the peak, by an eye at a fair height of 65 inches from the ground ; behind the circle the peak is seen below the horizon. From both these reasons, it seems nearly certain that the point of observation was intended to be from behind the trilithon, to the peak of the Heel stone ; as any place between the entrance and the trilithon shares the disadvantages of the former.

There can also be no doubt that the first appearance, and not the middle or completion of sunrise, was to be observed, as only the first appearance could coincide with the Heel stone at any possible epoch of erection.

The question then narrows itself to the epoch of the azimuth of sunrise being at $1° 24'$; this is equal to $9'$ change of declination from the present; and hence the sun rose over the peak of the Heel stone at 730 A.D. The probable error of this direction may be taken as about $2'$ from all causes; and the observed azimuths of sunrise may easily vary $3'$, by a change of $15°$ Fah. and $\frac{1}{2}$ inch barometer, and—considering permanent climatic changes— $1\frac{1}{2}'$ might be taken as a probable error. Thus a change of $3\frac{1}{2}'$ of azimuth would be about the probable error, and this would equal $1\frac{1}{2}'$ of declination, or about 200 years of time. So the final result, by the theory of sunrise observations, is limited to

$$730 \text{ A.D.} \pm 200 \text{ years,}$$

or perhaps as early as 400 A.D., considering climatic changes.

And at 100 B.C. the sun would rise east of the peak of the Heel stone $16'$, or about its own radius, an amount probably quite perceptible to the builders, considering the accuracy with which important parts of the work are laid out.

The large numbers of people that keep up with much energy the custom of seeing the sun rise at midsummer, somewhat suggests that it is an old tradition; and hence that it has some weight, independent of the mere coincidence.

The two other stones on the earth circle, 91 and 93, cannot have any connection with the solstitial risings or settings, as has been asserted.

-----

8. Sequence shown by Construction.

From the mean circles shown on Plate I., and their centres, there are important deductions to be made. The centre of the earth circle differs from the three stone circles very much more than they vary among themselves; and the difference (3 feet) is far larger than even the mean error of the circle, much more the probable error. Hence it is not likely that the stone circles were constructed at the same time as the earth; as, if so, the same centre would have been retained; and the earth cannot be later, as it is too good a circle not to have been struck on clear ground. Next, looking at the stone circles' centres, we see they are clearly different one from the other; this also suggests that this part of the work was not done all at once. Which preceded, the bluestone or sarsen? By this evidence, certainly the sarsen, as its error is but small;

whereas the outer bluestone circle has a large error, suggestive of being struck irregularly, after the trilithons were placed. The inner bluestones emphasise this, as nothing could come in the way in striking their semicircle, and they are accordingly as accurate in proportion as the sarsens.

We thus see by the centres that the bluestones were probably later than the sarsens; and as they never were a complete circle, shown by their pairing, it seems very probable that they were added at various times. The great want of uniformity (especially in the outer ones), some short, some long, some rounded; some flat, some squared; some shaped at the top, some naturally rough; some syenite, some schistose, some hornstone; all shows that they were executed at different times.

On examining the stones and mounds 91 to 94 on the earth bank in a similar manner, it will be seen that they are exactly opposite, stone to stone, and mound to mound. This strongly shows that they are contemporaneous; as is also shown by the fact that the diameters joining their centres cross each other at 45° 4′ ± about 6′, or just half a right angle; and further, the diameters are complementary to each other, being symmetrical about the axis of the structure, or at least about an axis differing only 18′ from the avenue. This shows also that the circle was divided into sixteenths, or $22\frac{1}{2}$°, as each diameter is $\frac{1}{16}$ from the right angles to the axis, or $\frac{3}{16}$ from the axis.

Further, the diameters both pass closer to the sarsen centre than to the earth circle centre (see Plate I.); the stones' diameter being one and a half times, and the mounds' diameter two and a half times, as far from the latter as from the former. This altogether implies, (1) that they were very carefully placed; (2) that there were probably not any other stones, certainly not a circle; (3) that the mounds and stones on the bank are contemporaneous, as matching in their position; (4) that they are certainly not earlier than the earth circle, or perhaps the avenue (as Hoare and others have supposed), and are probably not earlier than the sarsen circle. The small pits in the middle of each mound look much as if they had been ransacked when barrow digging was rife in the middle ages; and this would account for Hoare finding nothing in 92, and bones alone in 94.

We may observe that the earth circle appears to have been complete, and the avenue appended to it afterwards, judging by the arrangement of their junction.

Hence the concluded relative ages of the various parts are as follows: (1) Earth circle. (2) Avenue. (3) Sarsen circle, trilithons, mounds 92 and 94, and outlying stones, more or less contemporaneous. (4) Bluestones.

9. Sequence shown by Measures.

In 'Inductive Metrology' the principles of ascertaining whether a unit of measure was used in the construction of a building, and if so, what length the unit was, have been fully stated; and the methods there used may be applied here without further explanation. As we have seen that the different portions of the work are probably of different dates it is necessary to treat them all separately. On carefully comparing measurements of all the sarsens, especially of the most completely worked parts, it seems that no unit of measure was used in shaping them. But though the workers might very likely shirk adding so greatly to the trouble of squaring them, by also reducing them all to fixed sizes; yet this would not show that they might not attend to measurement, in placing them, where no great extra labour was required.

Taking the earth circle first, as giving more measurements for inter-comparison, the bank appears to have been equal in width to the ditch, reckoning on a small amount of spreading of the edges; thus the unaltered distance of the centres of bank and ditch apart gives the best indication of their width. This is 225 ± 4 inches. Now the crest of a bank, or the bottom of a ditch, is the least likely point to be metrical; the inner edge of the bank, the neutral point between it and the ditch, and the outer edge of the ditch, are the most likely points to be fixed in laying out the work on the ground. These three are respectively 3595, 4045, and 4495 inches diameter, allowing slightly for spread of edges. Applying then the 225-inch basis of the bank and ditch obtained above, we find these are 16, 18, and 20 of the unit, or radii of 8, 9, and 10, numbers very likely to occur. Taking 4046 ÷ 18 as practically the best defined, we obtain 224·8; but the most accurate result will be from the intermediate point, of 17 units diameter, on the crest of the bank; this is 3820 ± 2, ÷ 17 = 224·70 ± ·12. Next, how far is this applicable to other parts? The tumuli centres 92 and 94 are about 3391 apart, and the inner faces of the stones 91 and 93 estimated at 3376 (originally); the latter is better than the tumuli by far, and ÷ 15 = 225·1. Further, the radii of these tumuli are 218 ± 5, and 222 ± 6 inches. Considering the difficulty of estimating their ill-defined edges, this is very close to the unit, and the latter (94), which has a ditch, and is thus best defined, is the nearest to it.

On trying the sarsen circle neither the inner nor outer diameter agrees to this unit, and the trilithons and inner bluestones are equally intractable. The outer bluestones, which may be anything between 900 and 920 diameter, owing to the curved faces of the stones, are closely 4 of these units. The avenue measures seem as intractable as the sarsens. On trying the parallel banks they agree, their length east of the avenue centre being 13,570 inches, which ÷ 60 = 226·2 ; and west of the avenue 6800 inches, which ÷ 30 = 226·7. This agreement may be only casual, if there is any other evidence against it, as the breadths of the banks apart do not at all agree to this unit. On following westwards, to the portion in continuation of the same line, we find this 11,190 inches long, which ÷ 50 = 223·8. This brings us to the barrows, which are certainly ancient. It has been already mentioned that they are in a very nearly straight line, which suggests some accuracy. The distances of the centres apart are, from the second to the third, just double of that from the first to the second, which equals the distance of the third to the fourth. This length, thus thrice repeated, is 2262 ± 10 inches, and this is 10 of the unit found before in the earth circle. The diameters of the mounds are also closely 5 of this unit, but accuracy is impossible owing to their spreading. Taking up now the sarsens and inner bluestones, the outer sarsens are 1167·9 ± ·7 diameter, and the inner bluestones 472·7 ± ·5 inches diameter ; these quantities are very nearly as 10 : 4. The former has been recognised as 100 Roman feet, the latter is therefore 40 feet.* The foot by this would be 11·72, or 11·68 by the sarsens alone. The arrangement of the trilithons is obscure ; each of the pairs have their inner faces in a straight line, but there is no scheme sufficiently consistent and distinct to be worth entering on here.

To sum up, there are two units shown. One in the earth circle and its mounds and stones (91–94), and also in the line of barrows, and perhaps the parallel banks. This is, by the best elements, 224·8 ± ·1 inches, excluding the barrows, which give 226·7. In 'Inductive Metrology' I have shown that there is evidence, from entirely different materials, for a prehistoric mean unit of 22·51 ± ·02 inches, probably of Phœnician origin. The close agreement of this with 10 × 22·48 ± ·01 is striking. The other unit, the foot of 11·68 or 11·72, is as closely accordant with the Roman foot, which, though 11·64 in Rome, had a mean value of 11·68 ± ·01 in Greece, Africa, and England. Not that this shows Stonehenge to be post-Roman, as the unit was the great Etrurian and Cyclopean unit, originally derived from Egypt, and it may have been introduced at any date into Britain.

* This rather differs from the statements in 'Inductive Metrology,' as I had not so fully examined the details, and was fettered with the idea of the whole structure being of one epoch, in those statements.

10. Objects found.

It seems desirable to give a brief classified summary, mainly from Hoare, of all the objects found at Stonehenge. These are as follows :—Horns of stags and oxen, rotten bones of men or stags (Duke of Buckingham, 1620)*; heads of oxen, and other animal bones (Stukeley); parts of head and horns of deer, and other animals (Hoare); fragments of stags' horns under No. 95, bones alone in 94 (Hoare) Cover of incense cup, at 3 feet deep near trilithon (Inigo Jones); fragments of Roman and coarse British pottery (Hoare); coarse half-baked pottery at 6 feet deep by altar, and in ditch; bit of fine black Roman pot in hole of 57–58 trilithon; Roman pot at 3 feet deep by altar (Cunnington); Roman tile and mortar (Dr. Parkes). Charcoal, 6 feet deep by altar, and in ditch (Cunnington); by altar (Duke of Buckingham, 1620). Batterdashes, heads of arrows, armour eaten out by rust (of iron?) (Duke of Buckingham); large barbed iron arrow-head (Hoare). Plate of tin, with unknown letters, found under Henry VIII. (might this possibly be turned up now in some obscure collection?). Bactrian coin of 200 A.D., "found by a countryman at Stonehenge" (Southampton Museum).

---

11. Summary of Evidences on pre-Roman Age.

Besides dividing these evidences into pre- and post-Roman, some in each class are also applicable to a mixed origin, partly of each period.

By the details of the centerings we have seen that there are probably three main epochs in the work; those of the earth, sarsen, and bluestone circles; by their differences of centres they probably were arranged at some considerable intervals of time, and this almost precludes a post-Roman origin for the whole, as the Britons certainly had not a century of undisturbed possession after Hengest's slaughter.

The evidence of the measures shows two periods: that of the earth circle and barrows on the 22·5 inch unit, which is probably of Phœnician origin; and a second period, of the sarsens and inner bluestones, in which a different unit of 11·7 was used. The outer bluestones fitting to the 22·5 unit is not a coincidence of much weight, as they are so irregular,

---

* The place in Camden's print, dated 1575, where "men's bones are dug up," is outside the trench behind No. 27 : but the trench is drawn so close to the stones, that the spot is not really farther than the tumulus 94. It might possibly refer to the group of barrows out behind No. 19.

and the diameter is so uncertain; this also showing that they were not so likely to be metrical; thus the evidence of their centering outweighs this. This variety in the units points to a protracted erection, and the identity of the earlier unit with that of the group of barrows only containing bronze, glass, and bone, is of similar effect.

The care with which details are executed, especially the exactitude of erecting the stones; the great labour and time required to cut the blocks into shape; and the large quantity removed in surface work, in working the flat faces, and the flat ends and tenons; all these points are evidence of the length of time during which the work was carried on; and, with the signs of incompletion already mentioned, suggest that it occupied considerable time, and was at last dropped for want of materials or interest. The irregular distribution of the pairs of bluestones, and their diverse shapes, is another sign of gradual and irregular addition. All these points, like the first mentioned, are against a post-Roman origin.

An evidence of the pre-barrow age of the avenue, long ago noticed, is the gap in the line of barrows in the direction of the east branch of the avenue. Another token of this is in the parallel banks; these are certainly later than the avenue, by their crossing over it, and yet they run over a barrow and its ditch without effacing it, as if respecting the barrow; suggesting that the barrow was not worthless when they were made; also the western part is very nearly symmetrical about the barrow, as if it was arranged on purpose. These banks are worth more notice, unless they can be clearly shown to be recent, against which there are the reasons already mentioned. The highest objects found in these barrows are bronze spear-heads (2), a bodkin, and glass and amber beads.

Another proof of pre-barrow date, is the occurrence of chips of bluestone in the west barrow of the group west of Stonehenge, accompanied by a bronze spear-head and pin; and chips of both sarsen and bluestone in the bell barrow east of Stonehenge. With regard to the evidences connected with barrows, though very possibly some of them may be of Saxon date, like those in Kent and elsewhere, yet in none of those on which the arguments specially hinge has any iron been found; whereas iron continually occurs in Saxon barrows.

Another evidence brought forward is the collection of the barrows near Stonehenge; and this has been met by a counter-assertion, that the barrows are clearly not arranged about Stonehenge. Both are true, for though none of the barrows are grouped with any reference to it, yet they are thick in the neighbourhood, but not thickest close to Stonehenge, nor placed in sight of it. For on the Ordnance Map (filling some small groups by detailed plans) there are

Within ⅓ mile	17 barrows	= 22	per square mile.	
⅓ to 1 ,,	89 ,,	= 38	,,	
1 to 1½ ,,	92 ,,	= 23	,,	
1½ to 2 ,,	66 ,,	= 12	,,	
2 to 3 ,,	74 ,,	= 4·7	,,	
3 to 5 ,,	87 ,,	= 1·7	,,	

But it must be remembered that barrows are seldom or never grouped together, around a central one, or in any regular way; except a straight line, in a few cases. Hence they would not be likely to be arranged about Stonehenge in any case, though they ought to be thickest close to it, if they did refer to it.

The road running past Stonehenge points to a pre-Roman date. The details are given in "Notes on Roads," in the 'Archæological Journal,' 1878, which may be summarised thus:—The road cutting across the avenue askew, close to the circle, is certainly later than the structure, and made when it was disregarded. This road is an important highroad from Andover to Heytesbury, and on to Bristol, and it makes three sharp bends to avoid the great camp at Amesbury, instead of gently sweeping round it, the two portions on either side being in a continuous line. These bends show that it originally ran over the hill and was diverted by the camp. On this bent portion Amesbury has sprung up. This strongly shows that it is an old British road, like many now used (its slightly curved course is just of the character of such), and that it was altered probably at the Roman occupation, certainly not much later, as Amesbury (probably a pre-Saxon town) was built on its changed course. This points to a long pre-Roman date for the original course, and to a more remote time for Stonehenge itself. It has been objected that the present road is only a surveyor's arrangement of the end of the last century. But (beside the fact that Amesbury and Andover must always have had a communication westwards) it is shown in exactly the present course on the earliest road maps, of Seale (1748) and Kitchin (1747). Stukeley's drawings of 1723 also show a road, but close behind Stonehenge; this position is a mistake, as there is no trace of any road visible behind, only a faint single pair of ruts, such as might be made in a few days by a cart running up to the adjacent farm. Those who know how strongly old highroads are scored into the downs, especially up a valley-side (and Stukeley makes this to be a very distinct highroad in his drawings), will see that it is impossible for any other line for this important road to have been in use near the present course, as there is no trace remaining even on the sloping ground to the east.

One important evidence is the total absence of all inscription, or even a cross; the signs on the lintel, No. 156, being a forgery of 1827. Now there is nothing to show that the Cornish were more civilised than the Romano-Britons; yet in Cornwall there are stones with well-cut Latin inscriptions, of about the same post-Roman date as has been assigned to Stonehenge; or of a century or two later, when they were less, rather than more civilised. And the bluestones, if brought from Cornwall, would be obtained from people well used to lapidary inscriptions.

A similar evidence, though shadowy, is that of the plate of tin, found under Henry VIII. This was inscribed with characters which no antiquary of that age could read. If these had been Roman letters which were used by the Romano-Britons in Cornwall), or any derivative of them, it would have been intelligible; hence it would seem to have been in an Ogham, Runic, or Eastern alphabet, and in such a locality, probably, pre-Roman.

The weathering of the stones has been considerable, apart from artificial damage; the imposts, 152 and 154, are grooved out to 10 inches deep, and though these may be exceptionally soft, yet others show much change. But on the top of 60, which has certainly been exposed for over three centuries (see Camden's view), and perhaps much longer, there is scarcely any perceptible change, though the rain would lie on it, and favour disintegration. Certainly the cut surfaces of other stones seem, by their appearance, to have been exposed more than five times as long as No. 60.

An incidental point is that Stonehenge, by its tenons and mortises, is an evident imitation of wooden architecture; and as such, is more likely to belong to pre-Roman times, when wood was probably more used, than after the extensive stone and tile buildings of the Romans.

---

12. Summary of Evidences on Post-Roman Age.

The principal evidence for the post-Roman age is that of the Chroniclers, and this is so important that, although often discussed already, a brief summary of them seems requisite.

Though the modern horror of myths has led to the rejection of much of their history, because tainted with the fabulous; yet, besides accidental mistakes, we must draw a wide line between embellishments of true actions, and pure inventions. Most moderns are addicted to the former, though few may be guilty of the latter.*

The two detailed authorities are Nennius (circ. 850), and Geoffrey of Monmouth (circ. 1140), who professedly wrote from a certain Celtic MS. chronicle; Giraldus (1187) alludes to the same facts. They agree that about 462 A.D. the Britons and Saxons, after drawing a treaty, met at Amesbury for its ratification, and that the former were treacherously massacred: Nennius adding that there was a feast, and that the slaughter took place when the Britons were intoxicated; this is extremely probable, as nothing would be more likely than a feast on such an occasion, and the Saxons would wish for it (and are said to have proposed it) in order to begin the attack at better advantage. The convent where they met was "in the mountain of Ambrius." Now Stonehenge is on tolerably plain ground, and there is no likelihood of buildings having existed there, but by far the most likely place for a monastery would be on the steep hill just over Amesbury, known as Vespasian's Camp,† which probably contained perfect buildings of Roman period at that date. Next, after the slaughter, they were buried in a burying place near the monastery—observe, not at the monastery; and Aurelius erected the monument on the spot where they were buried. These points are quite consistent, a feast would not be held out in open country, but in a town. They met then for a ratification festival, in some buildings on Vespasian's Camp; there the Saxons massacred the Britons, and the latter were carried out to the spot then known as a burying place, *near* Amesbury, and there interred. And on this spot Aurelius Ambrosius afterwards erected a monument.

Now an incidental invention is seldom carried out and referred to in incidental allusions

---

* Eponymic derivations are considered fatal objections to historic veracity, and Isaac Taylor boldly says, "When we read in the Saxon Chronicle that Portsmouth derives its name from a Saxon chieftain of the name of Port, who landed there, we conclude at once that the name of Port is *eponymic;* or, in other words, that no such personage ever existed." Yet our nobility have their usual names from places. If this canon is held by future historians, and if some writer makes the jumble that Wellington and Melbourne in England, as well as at the Antipodes, are called after those premiers, our modern history will be credited as little as the Chroniclers are now. What is more natural than that the surname by which a barbaric invader was known should be the name of the place he first occupied? And it is a venial mistake to invert the order of derivation. The historical existence of Wihtgar (to take Taylor's other case) need not be doubted from his name, any more than the existence and deeds of the nobles known as Suf*folk* and Nor*folk* in later history. Latham says of these cases, "The names of Port and Wihtgar give us the *strongest* facts in favour of the suggested hypothesis, viz. the *ex post facto* evolution of personal names out of local ones."

† Only a name of Stukeley's.

in subsequent accounts, whereas this is thrice mentioned again. The previous account is in book vi. chap. 15, and viii. 12 of Geoffrey. In viii. 16, Aurelius is said to be buried near the convent of Ambrius, within the Giant's Dance. In viii. 24, Uther Pendragon was buried close by Aurelius; and again, in xi. 4, Constantine was buried close to Uther, in Stonehenge. All this is very consistent in general, and also in the detailed difference of "near" and "within" also, a different expression is used in each case, which does not look like repeating a conventional formula, or copying from one entry to another.

Another allegation against the historical character of the narrative is the interference of Merlin. But though his life (or their lives) are embellished elsewhere, in this incident there is nothing of which a modern contractor need be ashamed. He is only said to have used "the engines that were necessary" to remove the stones in Ireland to the ships, and they were brought over in the most matter-of-fact manner. Giraldus similarly says that by aid of his engines he took down the stones with incredible ease to bring them over for the erection of Stonehenge.

In short, in these accounts there is no discrepancy, and nothing to tax our credulity; and if other evidences should indicate that, by a very natural aggrandisement, the whole was ascribed to the authors of a portion, it is a fault that has often occurred in later writers, and which modifies, but not destroys, their testimony.

The other literary references are: (1) The circular temple of Apollo, mentioned by Hecatæus, which, if referring to Britain, might apply to any of the megalithic circles. (2) The Welsh triads, which, if genuine, need not in this case be pre-Roman. (3) Cuhelyn (circ. 550) says that the meeting of the Saxons and Britons "was in the precinct of Iôr, in the fair quadrangular area of the great sanctuary of the dominion." The epithet quadrangular is very irreconcilable. Hoare connects it with the cursus, but it seems inapplicable. Does it refer to square buildings in Vespasian's Camp, or to the camp itself, to which we have just seen the chronicles seem to point, and which might be reckoned in one property with Stonehenge? (4) Aneurin (circ. 550) mentions the "stone cell of the sacred fire," and the "great stone fence of the common sanctuary," which last seems very applicable to Stonehenge. One most important point in these last evidences is the attention they show to have been bestowed on megalithic remains in post-Roman times, which renders the more likely their erection or amplification at that period.

The frequent finds of Roman pottery are not conclusive, as they may have been dropped accidentally after the erection.   The pieces found at 3 feet deep by the altar, and the piece of tile raked out by a gamekeeper from a hole *under* one of the stones, and obtained by the late Dr. Parkes, as I am informed, are the most satisfactory.   Careful and intelligent digging is much needed to settle this.   The diameter being 100 Roman feet has been already mentioned to be no proof of age, as this unit was used for the early Cyclopean buildings of Greece and Italy.

The finds of iron are important.   Hoare's arrow-head may be of late date, lost accidentally; but the armour found in 1620, from being eaten through with rust, must almost certainly have been of iron, especially as Celtic bronze armour is unknown, and this almost proves post-Roman burial.   What especially emphasises these finds of iron, is, that no bronze is recorded to have ever been found there, and if wholly or mainly belonging to a bronze-using people bronze ought to be more frequent than iron.

The assumed low state of the pre-Roman inhabitants has been adduced as a proof that they could not have erected Stonehenge.   But their state has been much exaggerated ; or rather what was written of a few has been applied to all.   A thick population, accustomed to agriculture and trade, using metallic currency, and familiar with working in metals, appears to have occupied the southern counties.   The abundance of field-terraces, on ground which does not now pay for cultivation, all over Salisbury Plain and other barren downs, corroborates the statements of the Roman writers.

The evidence of the arrangement of the barrows has been fully entered on in the previous pages.

It has been said that the builders destroyed two barrows in making the earth circle, which must therefore be of a much later age; but the connection of these barrows with the circle has been here shown to be intentional.

The evidence from the azimuth of midsummer sunrise has also been fully stated, and shown to point to a post-Roman date ; and, if the solar reference be granted, the pre-Roman date would require us to suppose that the builders disregarded an error of at least half the diameter of the sun, which is unlikely.

The negative evidence, that no mention of Stonehenge or other such monuments is found in Roman writers, is worth very little, considering the remarkable omissions that occur in the most careful of the ancient topographers and historians.

13. Summary of Evidences on the Use.

By the examination of the details of the construction we have seen that the various parts are of different dates, and may therefore possibly be of different intention. The various theories propounded are either, (1) Sepulchral, (2) Memorial, (3) Religious, or (4) Astronomical; or combinations of some or all of these.

The Sepulchral may be taken as a certain element at some period, considering the instances of human bones reported in the sixteenth and seventeenth centuries, that the two tumuli are posterior to the earth bank, that Hoare found bones in one of them, and that Geoffrey repeatedly mentions burials. The name of the stone 96, called the Friar's Heel, with the absurd story of a heel mark in it, may have arisen from its being called the Heel stone, from Anglo-Saxon *hélan*, to hide or conceal, just as a cromlech at Portisham, Dorset, is called the Hel-stone. This would be probably from its covering a burial, as heal, hell, hele, all refer to horizontal covering. If it was used also for a vertical covering it might refer to its hiding the rising sun, as seen from the entrance.

The Religious intention is strongly contradicted by the absence of all traces of fire or calcination on the so-called "Altar stone," and by its very low position, almost flush with the ground; if any altar was there it can hardly be supposed (from its site) not to be this stone, which is, nevertheless, so unlikely. Another objection that has been raised is the assumed absence of wood at early dates. But Webb, in 1665, says (p. 188, ed. 1725) that from Amesbury to Stonehenge was a forest full of great trees, until two centuries before his time. This is not at all impossible, considering the flourishing woods that now exist on the chalk downs; and if some care be at present necessary to aid them in some cases, climatic changes might easily favour them more in former times, especially as a whole country being covered would affect the rainfall, and facilitate the growth of wood by checking the side pressure of wind. The absence of irregularity in the ground from the decay of large roots is, however, much against it. The lack of any carving on the stones is somewhat against a religious intention, as most religions have symbols; but it is no proof of hasty erection, as a hundred times the trouble requisite for it has been spent in shaping the stones. The repeated finds of stags' horns would seem to point to sacrifices or else to feasts, and confirm the statement of a forest having existed there.

The Astronomical theory has the strong evidence of the very close pointing to the midsummer sunrise, but apparently none other that will bear scientific scrutiny.

14. Concluding Remarks.

Having now stated all the facts and arguments, as far as I know them, I may be asked " What is your conclusion ? " I can only answer by giving due weight to each of the arguments somewhat as follows, and as no two persons will weight them alike, my readers must each weight them for their own satisfaction, as they may see fit.

	Pre-Roman date.		Mixed date.		Post-Roman date.	
	Pro.	Con.	Pro.	Con.	Pro.	Con.
Different dates, by centering	4	..	4	..	..	4
Different dates, by measures	3	..	3	..	..	3
Long in erection, by work	2	..	2	..	..	2
Gap in barrows for avenue	1	..	1	..	..	1
Barrows before banks	1	..	1	..	..	1
Chips in barrows	2	..	..	2	..	2
Road cutting avenue	4	..	3	1	..	4
Absence of inscription	4	..	..	4	..	4
Plate of tin	1	..	1	..	..	1
Weathering of stones	4	..	4	..	..	4
Chroniclers	..	8	6	2	8	..
Roman pottery	..	2	..	2	2	..
Iron objects, no bronze	..	3	..	3	3	..
Midsummer sunrise	..	4	4	..	4	..
No Roman account	..	1	..	1	1	..
Totals of weights, pro and con.	26	18	29	15	18	26

The weighting is done by considering what arguments would balance each other, and how far two or three poorer ones would balance a better. From this the preponderance is only 3 in 5 in favour of a pre-Roman, and against a post-Roman, date. A mixed date, some parts pre- and some post-Roman, satisfies the arguments somewhat better, reconciling 2 in 3 of them. This accordingly seems to be the most probable, and the least unlikely history of it would be :—1st. The earth circle made, like many other plain earth circles of great regularity in other places, for religious, sepulchral, or civil purposes. 2nd. The avenue added to it, pointing roughly to the sunrise. 3rd. Interments in the circle, in mounds, and under stones ; the sarsen trilithons and circle gradually erected ; the Heel stone placed to fix sunrise more accurately, when the trilithon was put up. 4th. The flat stone 95, and the altar stone 80, placed as tombstones over interments, carelessly, and somewhat askew. The neighbouring groups of barrows partly before and partly after this date; and interments at various dates in Stonehenge, because it was known as a burying place at the next epoch. 5th. In post-Roman times, the Britons massacred at Amesbury, and buried in Stonehenge. The uniform set of inner bluestones brought from Ireland by Merlin's skill, and erected in memory of them. 6th. Aurelius Ambrosius, Uther, and Constantine, and probably other chiefs, buried at intervals in Stonehenge; the rougher outer bluestones, which are of various characters and shapes, probably of various dates, and show less care and ability, erected to their memory. This outline, as a whole, seems to reconcile the various arguments more than any other; but I only regard it as the least unlikely supposition.

What is now necessary, to settle this much-disputed subject, is careful digging. By having a timber frame to carry the weight of a stone, clamped by its middle, it would be possible to remove the whole of the disturbed soil in layers from underneath each of the still erect stones, leaving the stone suspended; the earth being replaced and rammed, the stone would undergo no perceptible change, and could not be upset during the operation. The details of the work have been sketched out, and the whole frame would only cost a few pounds.

Another work, very urgently needed, is securing the great trilithon upright, 56, which now leans so much. This stone, from the evidence of various drawings, has inclined farther and farther since its first tip in 1620. In 1660 it was at 75°, in 1720 at 70°, in 1870 66°, and it is rapidly going over farther at present. On its fall, which cannot be far distant if unsecured, it will certainly break across, as it is cut unusually thin, has a large flaw in the middle, and will fall across its fallen lintel. To save this stone, the largest native hewn stone in England, and next to Cleopatra's needle in size, will be far better worth while than attempting to re-erect the fallen trilithon, which undertaking was mooted some years ago. It should be simply screwed and pulled back, rather askew, until it is upright, as this will probably restore it to its original place better than any other method. If some similar attention was given to a few of the outer circle stones that seem in peril at present, it would not be misplaced.

Many of the facts (particularly those of structural details), and half of the arguments, are here published for the first time; and the various references to the publication of the other facts and theories mentioned here, have not been given in detail, as the object was the structure, and not the history of its literature, which may be found in the pages of Inigo Jones, Dr. Charleton, John Webb, Stukeley, John Wood, John Smith, Sir R. C. Hoare, Dr. Fergusson, the Wilts Nat. Hist. Mag., and the Proceedings of the Archæological Societies. So much fresh evidence has appeared, on carefully examining the errors of construction, that it seemed requisite to embody it in a complete statement of all the arguments, especially as such a collection has not hitherto been published.

My best hope is that the arguments here brought forward and collected, will soon be rendered obsolete by a thorough investigation; though probably the plan will never be superseded by one of greater general accuracy, though perhaps small corrections may be made in it, as in all fallible work.

LONDON: PRINTED BY EDWARD STANFORD, 55 CHARING CROSS, S.W.

The plan of Stonehenge is only one of a series of considerably over a hundred surveys of earthworks and stone remains. It is proposed to publish selections of these at intervals, if there should prove to be a sufficient interest in them to defray their production. The most important, such as Chun Castle and village, Dawnsmaen, Boscawenoon, and other circles, Buttern Hill circle, Addington Stones, Fripsbury, Amphrey's Rings, Barbury, the Bishop's and All-Canning's Works, Steeple Langford, &c., would be taken first. Probably sections containing half-a-dozen plans, each of half a page of this size, and correct to about $\frac{1}{200}$ of an inch, with brief letterpress, would be the best arrangement. Any suggestions on this subject may be addressed to the author, Bromley, Kent.

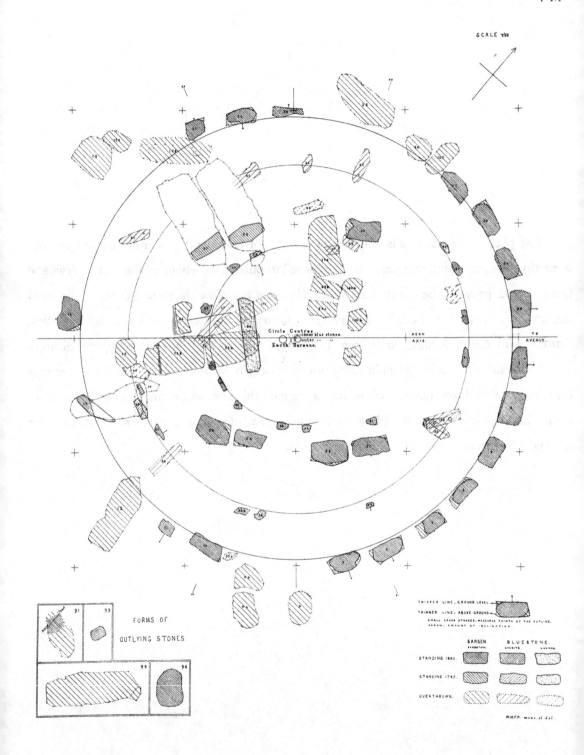

SCALE

Circle Centres {inner blue stones.
                {outer "
Earth Sarsens.

MEAN
AXIS

TO
AVENUE.

FORMS OF
OUTLYING STONES

91 93
95 96

THICKER LINE, GROUND LEVEL
THINNER LINE, ABOVE GROUND
SMALL CROSS STROKES, MEASURED POINTS OF THE OUTLINE.
ARROW, AMOUNT OF INCLINATION.

	SARSEN	BLUESTONE	
	SANDSTONE.	SYENITE.	VARIOUS.
STANDING 1880.			
STANDING 1747.			
OVERTHROWN.			

W.M.F.P. mens et del.

The figures of the ground-levels on Plate II. not having printed clearly, they are here re-stated; all above the bench-mark on the Friar's Heel.

	Inches.
At 350 inches behind No. 16	60·5
450 „ „ No. 54	53·7
150 „ „ Nos. 52–3	60·0
Mid between stone and earth circle, behind No. 52	31·5
Mid between stone and earth circle, behind No. 3	24·7
Mid between stone and earth circle, behind No. 29	32·3
700 inches behind No. 25 ..	44·1
Mid between stone and earth circle, behind No. 23	58·5
100 inches behind No. 57 ..	68·5
Between Nos. 48 and 29..	63·7
„ Nos. 32 and 3	43·3
„ Nos. 70 and 59 a	56·8
Lowest point of middle, 130 N.E. of altar ..	46·3

Middle of upper side of altar stone, 80	60·0
Mean level of tops of circle stones	213·3
Mean level of tops of circle lintels	241·7

Pl. III

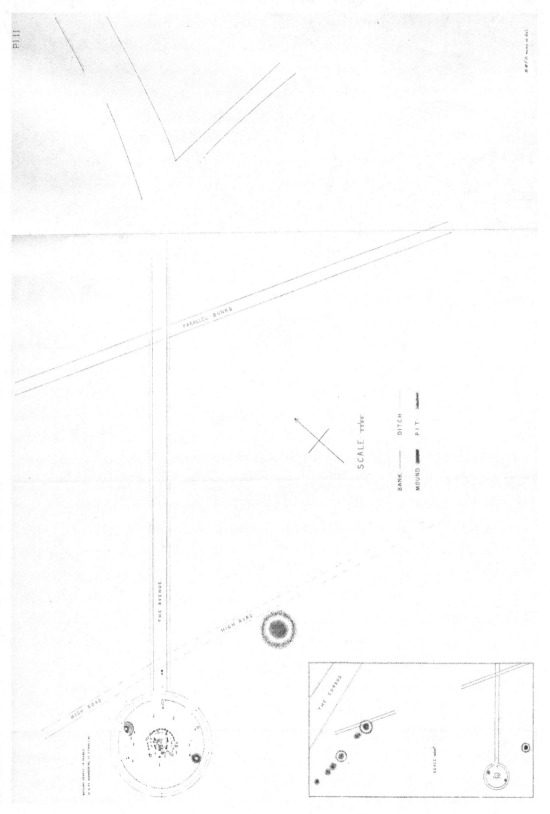

PARALLEL BANKS

THE AVENUE

HIGH ROAD

HIGH ROAD

SCALE

BANK.
MOUND
DITCH
PIT

THE CURSUS

SCALE

The material originally positioned here is too large for reproduction in this reissue. A PDF can be downloaded from the web address given on page iv of this book, by clicking on 'Resources Available'.

TUMULI

WILTUNENSES;

A

GUIDE TO THE BARROWS

ON THE PLAINS OF

STONEHENGE.

BY

Sir RICHARD COLT HOARE.

PRINTED BY J. RUTTER SHAFTESBURY.

1829.

DEDICATION.

———

The following Pages are addressed to those, who in future times, may have the same means and inclination to prosecute these Researches into the Early History of the Aborigines of our Island; and if ever undertaken, I hope they will prove equally productive of health, pleasure, and information, to them, as they have been to me.

R. C. H.

STOURHEAD, 1829.

DISCITE POSTERI.

WHATEVER may have been our researches through life, we are bound to communicate them before our death, especially if they lead to any new or important information. Under such sentiments, I think it incumbent upon me to hand down to future ages the result of our labors in the investigation of the British Tumuli, which still remain in numbers on the downs of Wiltshire.

Till within these few years they have been but partially examined, and even then not scientifically. Thomas, Earl of Pembroke, aided by the learned Dr. Stukeley, opened a few—but it was reserved for Mr. Cunnington of Heytesbury, to investigate them in a much more perfect manner, and to ascertain, that although sepulchral deposits had been found in the *upper* part of the tumulus, yet that the *primary* interment was always placed on the *floor* of the barrow, and generally within a cist cut in the chalk.

The following pages are limited to the environs of Stonehenge, and the numbers have a reference to the plans and plates in my larger work of Ancient Wiltshire, which, from its size and price, can find its way only into few libraries. It will also be observed, that our operations were directed only to the west of Ambresbury, and that a very wide field of enquiry is left open on the eastern side of that town, to any future antiquary. Some groups, in-

deed, have been explored between Ambresbury and
Everley; but there are numerous tumuli still left
unopened in that district; and there is also a fine
group near Winterslow Hut, worthy of attention;
and the Newton barrows, near Ambresbury, would,
I think, prove productive.

SEPULCHRUM CESPES ERIGIT.

These three words most fully explain the nature
of a *Barrow*, or *Tumulus*, and the most ancient
and simple mode of sepulture adopted by most
nations in the earliest times; I do not, however, re-
collect of seeing any in Italy or Etruria, though
the funeral rites of the Romans corresponded, in
some degree, with those of the Britons; for they
burned their bodies and deposited the ashes within
a funeral urn, which was placed in one of the
niches in their family mausoleum.

That the barrows on the plains around Stonehenge are of very high antiquity, no one can doubt,
though I am inclined to think that those near
Abury, and others in Dorsetshire, bear an earlier
date.* But by finding chippings of the stones of
Stonehenge in some of the barrows, (see No. 16),
we know that the mound was raised *after* Stonehenge. We may also ascertain another fact, that
the barrows were raised *prior* to the coming of the

---

* Especially the very curious barrow opened by Mr. Miles, and
described under the title of Deverel barrow.

Romans in our island, for the urns are all formed of unbaked clay, scratched over with instruments of bone, and not one of them turned by the lath; not one coin, nor one letter, has been found in them.

I have another reason for supposing these barrows to have been of a later period than some others at Abury, &c., as I perceive a greater variety of form in them, and more fancy in their ornaments.

Of these I think the following are marked decidedly:

1.—The Long Barrow, in point of dimensions, claims the first place; but not in its contents; for they have generally produced only skeletons interred without arms or urns, at the most elevated end of the barrow. One would think that they were intended as burial places for the common people: but why raise such immense mounds? Our researches in them having always proved so very unproductive, we latterly paid no attention to them.

2.—Bowl-shaped Barrow.—This is by far the most common shape; and on the noble ridge-way between Dorchester and Weymouth, I hardly distinguished any other amongst the numerous tumuli that abound on that fine eminence.

3.—This is the most beautiful of all the tall barrows, being moulded in the shape of a bell, and surrounded by a vallum.

4.—Druid Barrow; so called by Dr. Stukeley, and therefore let it retain its name; though I think the Druids had no claim to it, but rather the females, as we generally find beads, and other small ornaments in them appropriate to that class.

5.—POND BARROW.—The origin and history of this barrow has never been proved; nor will it ever be, except some future antiquary should turn up the *entire* area, with the hopes of finding out if it was intended for sepulchral uses or not.

MODE OF OPENING BARROWS.

Two methods have been adopted; either by cutting a channel directly *through* the mound, or by sinking a shaft down the centre, from top to bottom. We have adhered to the *latter* mode, with a view of not injuring the external form of the barrow; and by the care we have always taken in refilling them, they, even now, almost bear the appearance of not having been opened: but lest any of these should, at a future period, be explored, we have left in several of them tokens in lead and copper, stating they had been investigated.

I have before observed, that the barrows opened by Lord Pembroke and Dr. Stukeley, were very imperfectly investigated; for as soon as they found any sepulchral deposit near the *top* of the barrow, they thought the end was accomplished, and they made no further researches. But it was reserved for a later age, and for the intelligent mind of Mr. William Cunnington, to prove that the *primary* interment was not near the *top*, but always on the *floor* of the barrow, as that was chosen for the interment: a cist was dug in the chalk, the skeleton, or ashes, deposited, and the verdant mound heaped over the deceased; subsequent deposits were frequently made in the same tumulus. I cannot describe this system of burial better than by the lines of the poet Homer, who, in recording the obsequies of Patroclus, says

> " The Greeks obey! where yet the embers glow,
> Wide o'er the pile the sable wine they throw,
> Next the white bones his sad companions place,
> With tears collected in a golden vase,
> The sacred relics to the tent they bore,
> The urn a veil of linen * covered o'er,
> That done, they bid the sepulchre aspire,
> And cast the deep foundations round the pyre;
> High in the midst they heap the swelling bed
> Of rising earth, memorial of the dead."
>
> Iliad, Book xxiii.

Such was the sepulchral mound of the illustrious Greek, and such was that of the more humble Briton.

On arriving at the cist, particular care must be taken in digging, more especially if the rim of an urn appears above the surface; and in that case you must proceed very slowly and carefully around

---

* We have frequently found the veil of linen covering the ashes fastened by a brass pin.

the edge of the cist, so as to leave the urn so detached, as to be able to remove it entire; at first we made use of a mason's trowel for that purpose, but found afterwards that a knife with a very strong blade was more effectual, and had some made at Salisbury for that purpose, of this pattern:

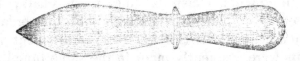

Blade 7 inches by 2, in the widest part, handle 5 ditto.

ON SEPULCHRAL URNS.

URNA TEGIT CINERES.

Having detailed our mode of opening barrows, I shall now proceed to describe the different systems of burial.

There appear to have been four distinct modes of interment.

1.—The skeleton with the legs and knees gathered up to the chin.

2.—The skeleton extended at full length.

3.—The body burnt, and the bones and ashes placed within an urn, and covered by a linen cloth fastened by a small brass pin; the mouth of the urn upwards, and sometimes protected by a flat stone at top, as in tumulus and plate 1.

4.—The same form of interment, with this difference, that the urn was inverted over the bones, as in plate 2, which resembles an egg put into a basket.

But these urns varied in form, size, and decorations. They were all made of unbaked clay, and many of them bear the black marks of the funeral fire. We have never found any other of the upright form; and the superior size of the one figured in plate 1, which was preserved entire, and measured 22½ inches in height, and 15 inches in diameter. (No. 14.)

In the Deverel barrow opened by Mr. Miles, there were several of this shape, but of much ruder make, and much blackened by fire.

Plate III describes an urn of a very different form, and much more decorated; these I have named *drinking cups*, which were placed near the corpse, and supposed to contain a viaticum for the dead; a custom which still prevails in distant countries.

In plate IV we see urns or cups of a very different form and pattern, richly ornamented with a variety of patterns, especially that styled, "The grape cup." These I have denominated *Incense cups;* for which purpose I conclude they were used, as we find in most of them holes for suspension.

How singularly do all these circumstances correspond with the lines quoted from Homer. The funeral pile, the raising the mound of earth, the deposit of the ashes in a vase, and the burning of fragrant oils over the tomb.

It is necessary to observe, that the zigzag pattern is the one most generally adopted on the urns; and especially on the handle of the spear or dagger No. 158, whioh is a most wonderful piece of art, the whole pattern being worked with gold pins of the most diminutive size.

Let us now consider what articles were found deposited either in the sepulchral urns, or in the cist. We learn from Cæsar, that the Gauls were in the habit of depositing with the dead those articles which were esteemed the most valuable to them in life. "*Omnia quæ vivis cordi fuisse arbitrantur in ignem inferunt, etiam animalia.*" Of which similar custom we have many proofs amongst the Britons.

The articles so deposited, were celts of flint and of brass; spear heads and arrow heads of flint; also daggers of brass gilt; with various other articles of the same metal. The smaller articles were beads of amber, jet, &c.; very small lance heads of brass; armillæ of ivory and bone; pointed skewers of bone, with which they scratched the rude ornaments on their vases; and whet-stones, with which they sharpened these skewers. In a few barrows, viz. No. 155 & 158, we found ornaments of thin and very pure gold.

Amongst these various articles we may trace the rude implements of the Britons in bone and flint; and the more polished works of some more civilized nation in the articles of gold, brass, beads, &c. We are but little conversant in the history of the early inhabitants of our island; but from the situation of their residences on our exposed downs, we have reason to think they resembled the Nomades of antiquity, who wandered from place to place subsisting on the produce of their herds, and of the chace. That the country abounded in deer of an immense size, is proved by the numerous specimens of horns found in the barrows; and it is singular that we meet with so few bones of sheep and horned cattle. The beautiful arrow heads of flint, point out their instruments of destruction before the use of iron was known. I have frequently asked, "Where did they get their water?" as many of their settlements were far distant from any river; but this is a question I cannot satisfactorily answer.

BRITISH SETTLEMENTS.—When we behold so many memorials of the dead dispersed over the extensive plains around Stonehenge, we are naturally led to inquire, Where were the residences of the living? This question I am able to answer in a satisfactory manner; for we have discovered those spots which they had selected for their habitations; and the merit of this discovery is solely due to Mr. Cunnington; for no other antiquary ever even ventured to make a conjecture on the subject; though they are so manifest on our downs, that in my History of South Wilts, I have noticed fifty of them. My readers will naturally ask for evidence and proofs; and my answer will be, "the spade;" for on turning up the turf on those places where we found it more verdant and full of cavities, we invariably dug up a richer and blacker mould, animal bones, charcoal, and fragments of pottery; the certain indication of former habitation. The Britons probably lived in huts covered with leaves or straw, for stone could not be found on our downs; but during my researches in North Wales, I saw some very perfect specimens of British huts on the summit of Pen Maen Mawr; they were circular, formed of stone, without cement, in the form of a cone, with a small entrance, resembling the huts of the Hottentots.

Of these ancient British settlements, there are four examples within the district I am describing.

The first and second are on the road leading from Ambresbury to Shrewton, a little beyond the Devizes road, where we find two decided British works, one to the north, the other to the south of the turnpike road; they seem to have been connected by a ditch or covered way; the one to the south is the most perfect, for we can trace the square form, and the lines of the streets and cavities, where the huts or houses stood.

The third is at Durrington Walls, advantageously situated near the banks of the river Avon.

The fourth is to the west of the Lake group of barrows, from whence an ancient bank and ditch run in a direct line to the British settlements on Winterbourn Stoke Down, seeming to form a connection between them. These banks and ditches are frequent on our downs, and as they generally led to a British village, I am inclined to consider them as covered ways leading to and from the settlements.

Having stated the nature of our Wiltshire tumuli, the mode of opening them, &c., I shall now give a faithful account of the deposits found within them; the greater part of which may be seen, in a high state of preservation, in my Wiltshire Museum, which is always open for inspection.

INDEX

TO THE BARROWS ON THE PLAINS AROUND STONE-
HENGE, CORRESPONDING WITH THE ACCOUNT OF
THEM IN THE HISTORY OF ANCIENT WILTSHIRE.

Page	No.	
		NOTE.—The numerals commence from the west, on **Winterborne Stoke Down,** near two British villages.
117	1	Interment of burnt bones.
	2	Prior opening.
	3	A long barrow, 104 feet by 64 feet, burnt bones mixed with mortar.
	4	Prior opening.
118	5	Appears to have been a family sepulchre; several deposits of skeletons; a small drinking cup; a large black cone, &c.
	6	Prior opening.
	7	A fine bell-shaped barrow; missed the interment; but fragments of an urn and bones indicated a prior opening.
	8	Burnt bones; a piece of square stone, polished on one side, having two marks cut into it, and a whetstone.
119	9	An urn inverted, engraved in plate xvi; large stag's horns; also two skeletons. —N. B. In this barrow we see the two different modes of interment.

14

Page	No.	
119	10	In this barrow was found one of those vitrified beads, called the Glain neidyr, and which, I believe to be unique, engraved in plate xiv.
120	11	A pond barrow.
		We now come to a fine group of barrows at the intersection of the road leading to Devizes, amounting to 27.
121	1	A long barrow.
	2	Burnt bones and a small urn.
	3	Near the top was a rude urn enclosing burnt bones; but we missed the primary interment.
	4 5 6	} Simple interments by cremation.
	7	First interment: the skeleton of a child, with an urn; and in a cist beneath, the skeleton of an adult, with a drinking cup at its feet.
	8	A Druid barrow: burnt bones and a fine drinking cup
	9	A simple interment: burnt bones.
	10	Query. If sepulchral? nothing found.
	11	Burnt bones; a small cup, and a bone pin.

Page	No.	
121	12	A simple interment by cremation.
	13	Nihil.
	14	A pond barrow
122	15	An interment of burnt bones deposited in a box of wood; two small pieces of ivory, apparently the tips of a bow; a beautiful spear-head of brass, and another smaller; remains of brass rivets to the box, &c.; five skeletons were also found at a short depth below the surface of the mound.
	16	A very fine tumulus. A skeleton placed within the rude trunk of an elm tree; on the left side of its head a beautiful urn had been deposited, but crushed to pieces by the superincumbent earth; we were however, enabled to collect sufficient of the fragments to make a drawing of it, which is engraved in plate xv. This urn is different in shape from any we have found, and of a redder tint. Near the breast of the skeleton, lay a fine brass dagger, (No. 2, plate xv), which had been guarded by an ornamented scabbard of wood. Also an ivory pin with a handle; and another very perfect spear-head, very elegantly moulded, lying near the thigh, No. 4, plate xv. The contents of this barrow were so rich, that we named it King Barrow.
	17	A simple interment of burnt bones.

Page	No.	
123	18	Contains within its area three small tumuli, in each of which were interments of burnt bones. In the largest, which is in the centre, was a small urn and some large beads of amber; in the second, some beads; and in the third, only burnt bones.
	19	A sepulchral urn, (plate 16), with burnt bones, and under it a skeleton, and a perforated pebble stone.
124	20	A pond barrow.
	21	A prior opening.
	22	A skeleton.
	23 24	} Unproductive.
	25	A mixed deposit: skeleton, burnt bones, horns of deer, &c. Two small earthen cups neatly ornamented, near the head of the skeleton; a ring or bracelet of bone or ivory; two oblong beads of bone, and two whetstones; a brass pin; two petrified cockle shells, &c.
	26	A skeleton deposited within a cist, in a shallow case of wood, and boat-like form, round its neck was a great variety of amber and jet beads; a lance head; a brass pin, and a small neat urn, broken.
125	27	A very large tumulus: at the depth of two

Page	No.
125	27

feet, were the skeletons of two dogs; at the depth of seven feet, a sepulchral urn inverted, which lay in the lap of a skeleton; on removing this deposit, five more skeletons were found lying side by side, and at their head a drinking cup: thus we see interments made in this barrow at different periods.

Quitting the group of barrows on Winterborne Stoke Down, we proceed over the plain in an easterly direction, towards **126 12** Stonehenge, where we find a group of small tumuli; in one of which was an urn rudely baked, containing ashes, and two pieces of twisted brass wire, which probably once formed a ring; the other barrows had been ploughed over.

13 A Druid barrow, containing a simple interment of burnt bones.

14 A group of eight barrows of different sizes, close to the road side leading to Ambresbury. The tumulus nearest to that place produced the finest sepulchral urn we had yet discovered, and in a perfect state; it measured 15 inches in diameter at top, and $22\frac{1}{2}$ inches in height; it contained a deposit of burnt bones, which was protected by a large triangular stone placed over the mouth of the urn. It is engraved in plate xvi. The other barrows in this place produced nothing of importance.

On approaching Stonehenge we come

Page	No,	
		to a fine group of barrows, several of which had been much defaced by rabbits.
127	15	A Druid barrow with an interment of burnt bones.
	16	A mutilated flat barrow, which appears to have been one of those opened by Dr. Stukeley, and thus mentioned by him in his account of Stonehenge, as remarkable from containing chippings of the stones that formed the temple at Stonehenge, and thereby proving that this British barrow was raised subsequently to the grand pile of stones. "And in a very great and old fashioned barrow west from Stonehenge, I found bits of red and blue marble chippings of the stones of the temple; so that, probably, the interred was one of the builders, *(dubito)*."—Stukeley, p. 46. This barrow contained the bones of two skeletons which had been deposited on the floor, with animal bones, and several pieces of stag's horns, as well as some fragments of sarsen stones, similar to those of the great trilithons at Stonehenge.
	16	This barrow contained also an interment of burnt bones deposited in a fine circular cist, and with it was found a spear-head of brass in good preservation, and a pin of the same metal. We found also the chippings of stone mentioned by Stukeley.

Page	No.	
127	17	No discovery.
	18	Injured by rabbits.
	19	Seems to be one of those opened by Lord Pembroke or Dr. Stukeley.
	20	Had been opened and contained a skeleton.
	21 22	}These barrows proved unproductive.
	23	At his first trial Mr. Cunnington was unsuccessful, but on a second, he found a rude urn inverted over a pile of burnt bones, amongst which was an elegant pair of ivory tweezers.
		Quitting Stonehenge, and pursuing the road towards Ambresbury, we find three tumuli situated between the avenue and turnpike road.
159	24	A very flat barrow, in which were the skeletons of an adult and a child, deposited in a very shallow cist, which had been disturbed by a prior opening.
	25	A wide bowl-shaped barrow, contained a skeleton, with its head placed towards the north, a drinking cup by its right side, and near it, a neatly formed pin of bone.
	26	This tumulus is situated on the borders of the turnpike road, and produced a large

Page	No.	
159	26	interment of burnt bones; a cone of jet; 2 oblong beads of the same substance; 18 of amber, and a very small cone of the same.
	27	We now traverse the line of the avenue which once issued from Stonehenge, and find a solitary barrow which appeared to have had a prior opening, and to have contained the skeletons of two adults and two children. Round the arm of one of them was an ornamented bracelet of brass, which our labourers unfortunately broke.
160	29	On approaching the cursus we find a numerous continuation of barrows, flanking the southern side of it, the two first of which appear to have been opened by Lord Pembroke in the year 1722, and are thus mentioned by Stukeley;—"In the year 1723, by order of Thomas, Earl of Pembroke, I begun upon a barrow north of Stonehenge, in that group south of the cursus. It is one of the double barrows there, and the more easterly, or lower of the two. It was reasonable to believe that this was the sepulture of a man and his wife, and so it proved, at least of a daughter. About three feet below the surface, was a layer of flints about a foot thick, which rested on a layer of soft mould another foot, in which was an urn full of bones; it was formed of unbaked clay, of a dark reddish colour, and crumbled into pieces; it had been rudely wrought with small

Page	No.
160	29

mouldings round the verge, with circular channels on the outside, with several indentures between, made with a pointed tool.*

The remains seem to have been of a girl about 14 years old, and a great many female ornaments were intermixed with the bones; beads of all sorts, and in great number, of glass of divers colors, mostly yellow, one black; many in long pieces notched between, generally of a blue color; many of amber, of all shapes and sizes, flat squares, long squares, round, oblong, little and great; likewise many of earth, some little and white, many large and flattish like a button, others like a pulley, but all had holes to string through; many of the button sort seem to have been covered with metal, there being a rim worked in them, wherein to turn the edge of the covering; one of these was covered with a thin film of pure gold. These were the young lady's ornaments, and all had undergone the fire; a small javelin of brass was also deposited with this heroine, and a sharp bodkin which had a handle.†

We recomposed the ashes of this illustrious defunct, covered them with earth, leaving visible marks at top, of the barrow having been opened, to dissuade any other from again disturbing them, and this was our practice in all the rest."

* Of these bone tools sharpened at one end, I have several in my Museum.

† Specimens of all these articles may be seen in my Museum.

Page	No,
160	29

Note.—Mr. Cunnington having seen the before-mentioned account, did not attempt a second investigation of this barrow.

" Dr. Stukeley then opened the adjoining tumulus, and at the depth of 14 inches came to the entire skeleton of a man, whose body lay with the head towards the north, and all the bones were exceedingly rotten."

And here I must observe, that the learned Doctor finding an interment *above* the floor of the barrow, and supposing that he found the interment, desisted from further researches; but Mr. Cunnington being convinced that the *primary* interment was deposited *on*, or *beneath* the floor of the barrow, explored, in 1823, this tumulus, when at the depth of six feet, he came to the floor, which was covered with ashes, and on further digging he found a cist 18 inches deep, and within it, a complete interment of burnt bones, and with them six beads, apparently of horn, four of which were perforated, the other two were circular and rather flat, but all appeared as though they had been burnt.

162 30 A beautiful bell-shaped barrow, and the largest of this group, which from its superior size and beauty, raised our expectations of success; but alas! after immense labor, to the depth of 15 feet, we found only a simple interment of burnt bones, unaccompanied by urn, arms, or trinkets.

Note.—Experience has taught us that

Page	No.	
162	30	we must not judge of the *contents* by the *form* of a barrow. *"Fronti nulla fides."*
	31	Bowl-shaped·: produced an interment of burnt bones, with a small spear-head.
	32	A simple interment of burnt bones.
163	33	A Druid barrow, surrounded by a fine vallum, but without any elevation, as usual, in the centre; our workmen however luckily hit on the deposit of burnt bones, accompanied by a great many beads.
	34	A prior opening.
	35	We missed the interment.
	36	The contents of this barrow recompensed us, in some degree, for our failure in the two last. It produced three skeletons laid from north to south, and immediately one over the other, the first about two feet deep, the second on a level with the adjoining soil; close to the head of the last was a drinking cup, with a considerable quantity of something resembling decayed leather; six feet lower, laid the third skeleton, with which was found the drinking cup engraved in plate xvi; the teeth of this skeleton were perfectly white, and not one of them unsound, but the most remarkable circumstance was, a skull cut in half, and so nicely, as if done by a saw, for I hardly think a knife could have cut it asunder so minutely: it was re-interred.

Page	No.
163	37

In this barrow we found only black ashes and burnt bones.

38 We missed the interment after much labor.

39 This barrow had experienced a prior, but a partial opening, and one skeleton, with a drinking cup, had been disturbed. On reaching the floor we discovered another skeleton with its head due north, and a great quantity of beads, some of which being about the neek, we concluded it was the deposit of a female; close to the head was a kind of basin neatly ornamented, but fractured; on removing the head, we were surprized to find it resting on a drinking cup that had been placed at the feet of another skeleton, which also lay north and south; with this drinking cup were found a fine spear-head of flint, and a singular stone, which are engraved in plate xvii.

40 In point of size, this tumulus may be styled "the monarch of the plains," and its history and contents still remain veiled in obscurity; for we made two attempts on it, and in each were unsuccessful; some future antiquary may, perhaps, be more fortunate in finding the deposit.

164 41 An interment of burnt bones.

42 The same, with a brass pin and part of its handle, deposited in a neat and perfect urn, engraved in plate xvi.

Page	No.	
164	43	These two barrows are in a singular situ-
	44	ation, being raised in the centre of the cursus. Query.—Were they erected previous, or subsequent to the cursus? In the first of these were the skeleton of an adult with a drinking cup, and on the floor of the barrow that of a child; we afterwards found the third skeleton of a man lying with his head to the north, and close to it was a curious pebble, and under his left hand a brazen dagger.
	44	In the adjoining barrow we found only a simple deposit of burnt bones.
	45	The next barrows that occur in our iter
	46	westward, are three in number, in a line
	47	nearly parallel to each other. All of which proved uninteresting in their contents.
	48	A Druid barrow, containing burnt bones and a brass pin.
165	49	A long barrow.
	50	In this tumulus we felt much perplexity, although not uncommon, owing to the Britons having adopted so many different modes of burial. At the depth of five feet we found a regular stratum of flints intermixed with black vegetable mould, on removing which, we came to the floor of the barrow, in which some channels had been formed. One of these connected with a cist, contained a skeleton lying from south to north; in another

Page	No.
165	50

channel we found a large branch of a stag's horn; and in a little corner a shovel ful of bones; and near the feet of the skeleton lay a considerable quantity of very small bones of birds or mice. The day being far advanced, we did not pursue the other channels, which, probably, may have contained other skeletons, &c.

51 Two skeletons were found with their heads laid towards the north, the one an adult, the other a young person.

52 53 } Uusuccessful; nothing of importance being found.

54 A fine bell-shaped barrow, produced interments of burnt bones.

55 A simple interment of burnt bones.

56 Previously investigated, but we found an arrow-head of flint near the top.

Adjoining this group of barrows there are evident remains of another cursus, apparently unfinished, which has not been noticed by the former writers on Stonehenge.

57 to 65 We now proceed to another group of barrows situate to the north of the latter, and consisting of four Druid, and five circular tumuli, all of which appeared to have been opened some years ago by Mr. Cunnington, when no regular ac-

Page	No.	
165	65	count was kept of his discoveries, but from his rough notes I can collect that they contained small articles, viz. beads of amber and jet, a brass dart, ivory tweezers, articles of bone, and a whet-stone.
166	66	Fragments of a skull, of a large sepul-chral urn, and drinking cup.
	67	Like the former; seemed to have had a prior opening.
	68	A pond barrow.

On the opposite hill is a beautiful group of barrows, which, with a beautiful day, and attendance of many of our friends from Salisbury, cheered and enlivened our prospects, but we again had cause to exclaim, "*fronti nulla fides,*" for no arrow heads were found to mark the profession of the British hunter; no gilded dagger to point out the chieftain of the clan ; nor any necklace of amber or of jet to distinguish the British female ; and a few rude urns only marked the antiquity and poverty of those who had fixed on this spot as their mausoleum.

	69	Was opened at a prior period by Mr. Cun-nington.
	70	An interment of burnt bones deposited in a cist.
167	71	A Druid barrow, produced the skeleton

Page	No.	
167	71	of a child, near the surface; and lower down, two rude sepulchral urns, one above the other, each containing burnt bones.
	72	Produced a sepulchral urn.
	73	A Druid barrow, contained, near the surface, a skeleton, with four wooden beads near its neck.
	74	A Druid barrow with ashes in a cist.
	75 76 77 78 79	All these tumuli appear to have had a previous investigation, and to have been robbed of their contents.
	80	Not sepulchral.
	81	Contained a large rude urn, with burnt bones.
	82	Had two simple interments of burnt bones, just under the surface.
	83	Contained a sepulchral urn with a small brass pin. To the south of No. 80, on the opposite hill, is a Druid barrow, (not marked in the plan,) which contained a large rude urn.

In the same easterly direction but nearer to the cursus, is another fine group of barrows, equally inviting to the eye, but nearly as unproductive as the former.

Page	No.	
167	84	This is the largest of these tumuli, and has been ploughed over, we found in it pieces of stag's horns, pottery, the bones of a skeleton, two knives, and fragments of a drinking cup, but the primary interment was a skeleton with its legs gathered up, and hands placed under its head.
	85	Had contained an interment of burnt bones, but had been opened.
	86	Had also experienced the same investigation.
	87	A Druid barrow contained fragments of an urn, with burnt bones.
	88	Produced near the surface, fragments of a rude urn with burnt bones, and lower down a sepulchral urn reversed over a deposit of burnt bones.
	89	Has been in tillage, and contained a skeleton with its head towards the north.
	90	A large urn rudely ornamented, and inverted over a deposit of burnt bones
168	91	Burnt bones, ashes, and charred wood.
	92	On the floor of this barrow, we found the remains of a skeleton, fragments of a funeral urn, and some enormous pieces of stag's horns.
	93	Contained near the top a deposit of burnt

Page	No.	
168	93	bones, in a rude broken urn with a small cup, also the remains of a skeleton, charred wood, stag's horns, and pieces of apparently prepared for warlike instruments.

The primary deposit was a skeleton, accompanied by a very fine and richly ornamented drinking cup, in perfect preservation, engraved in plate xviii.

94 This barrow being sown with wheat, could not be investigated.

95
96
97 } All these barrows contained interments of burnt bones, and proved totally uninteresting.
98
99

A little further to the east we find another cluster of nine barrows, on the brow of a hill.

100 A simple interment of burnt bones.

101 A similar interment accompanied with two black rings of some bituminous substance, and one pretty bead.

102 A deposit of burnt bones, in a cist with remnants of the cloth in which the relics were enveloped.

103 A deep circular cist with ashes.

104 This barrow had been opened, and must have proved interesting to the first in-

Page	No.
168	104

vestigators, for we found the bones of several skeletons, fragments of urns, and a rude instrument made from a stag's horn.

105
106 } These barrows had been opened.

107 Produced a small deposit of burnt bones, a pile of ashes, and a pin of bone.

108 A pond barrow.

On a rising ground to the north, is another group of seven barrows, the exploration of which proved rather unsatisfactory.

109
110 } We found that all these three barrows
111 had been opened.

112 A double barrow; somewhat resembling a long one, but ditched all around. The lowest part had been opened, and contained an interment of burnt bones, in the other mound was a deposit of burnt bones, secured by a linen cloth under a rude urn.

113 Had been examined, but we found in it fragments of a skeleton and of an urn.

114 Burnt bones and ashes in a deep cist.

115 A similar interment, but had been opened.

I had for a long time viewed these two

Page	No.	
168	115	last groups with satisfaction, and anticipated much pleasure and success in opening them, but we are again doomed to disappointment.
		Adjoining the cursus there are six small barrows, which produced nothing of importance.
169	116	Had a prior opening.
	117	Contained a small rude urn and burnt bones.
	118	A small long barrow, with ashes and burnt bones in a cist.
	119	The same interment.
	120	A pond barrow.
	121	Contained a deposit of burnt bones with an inverted urn.
		We now approach the banks of the river Avon, where there once was a British Settlement, now bearing the name of Durrington Walls, and near it are a few tumuli.
	122	An elevated mound bearing the appearance of a barrow, but we dug in it to the depth of eleven feet, and found no marks of sepulture.
	123	The mutilated remains of an enormous Druid barrow.

Page	No.	
170	124	These three barrows have a singular appearance, as rising from one base, but I think that the barrow was originally a long one.—We opened the mound at the smallest end, and found only ashes, and charred wood; in the central lump, was a skeleton and a drinking cup, both of which had been disturbed; on the floor was a circular cist like a little well, but containing no deposit.
	125	In tillage.

Near these barrows is a large sarsen stone, said to have been dropped whilst carrying to Stonehenge, and there is also another lying in the river, both of which are in a direction between Stonehenge and Abury, from whence the stones forming the great trilithons are supposed to have been brought.

126
127 On approaching Vespasian's camp, we found two barrows near each other, which we did not attempt to open.

Before I quit that portion of the downs, north of the turnpike road, it is necessary to notice two groups of barrows, consisting of seven in each, and styled the old king and new king barrows, they are all placed in rows, and between the two rows, the avenue seems to have led from Stonehenge to this point, as a chasm is left open in the centre between the two rows; these barrows having a clump of trees on each of them,

Page	No.
170	127

have been hitherto untouched, but the time may come when they may be investigated, for I consider them as the most important mounds in the whole plain, and connected in some degree, with Stonehenge.

We must now turn our attention to the numerous barrows dispersed over the plain, to the south of the road leading from Ambresbury to Deptford; and the first that occurs is No. 128, which, together with No. 129, had experienced a prior opening; but in a cist of the latter, a lance-head of brass, had escaped unnoticed.

128

129

130 This barrow had been partially opened, but some of the interments remained perfect and attended with some novel circumstances. At a foot and a half below the surface we found a skeleton with a drinking cup, and lower down a deposit of burnt bones, on the east side lay the skeletons of two infants, each placed over the head of a cow or heifer, apparently of a small size; we afterwards found a cist cut in the chalk, to the depth of four feet, which contained the primary interment of a skeleton, but these relics had been disturbed, and some brazen articles removed with which the bones were tinged.

131 Had been opened by the neighbouring farmers.

Page	No.	
170	132	In this barrow was an unusual quantity of burnt bones, and with them two drinking cups. two incense cups, and two brass pins. One of these cups was preserved entire, and engraved the size of the original in plate xxiv.
199	133	Is a very high barrow, on which the plough has encroached. It contained within a deep cist, a pile of burnt bones, and a very beautiful and perfect grape cup, which was engraved full size, in plate xxiv.
	134 to 137	} All these barrows bear marks of prior openings.

NORMANTON GROUP.—We now come to a noble group of tumuli, running in a line from south-east to north-west, diversified in their forms, perfect in their symmetry, and rich in their contents.

	138	A Druid barrow, which had been opened.
	139	A mean looking barrow, which produced within a shallow cist, a pile of burnt bones, and with them two fine daggers of brass, a long pin of the same metal, in the form of a crutch, a whetstone, and a small pile of bones; the brass pin and whetstone are engraved in plate xxiv.
	140 to 143	} All these had been explored.

Page	No.	
199	144	Remains of a skeleton, head towards the north accompanied by a small lance-head of brass.

145 Appeared to have been opened, but we found in the cist a piece of ivory resembling the handle of a cup, and a large black pebble, shaped like a kidney.

146 Appears to have been the barrow opened by Stukeley, and marked B. in Tab. ix. of his work.

147 One of these two barrows, enclosed within the same ditch, was opened by Thomas Earl of Pembroke, in the year 1722, and is marked A. in Tab. ix. of Stukely, and described at page 44 of his description of Stonehenge; but experience having given us repeated proofs that the system of opening barrows was but imperfectly understood in former days, we determined to try our luck, and on reaching the floor, we discovered the primary cist, containing a deposit of burnt bones, with two articles of ivory engraved in plate xxiv.

In the smaller barrow Dr. Stukeley not finding the interment, left two half-pence, covered with stones, one of the reign of king William III, the other of George I, 1718, this last coin was in high preservation, after the lapse of 86 years. Still Mr. Cunnington, continued his researches, till he found a cist at the east end of the barrow, and

Page	No.	
199		an interment of burnt bones, with which were deposited four amber beads, two of jet with convoluted stripes, and a little broken cup.
201	148	Unproductive.
	149	A Druid barrow, had been opened.
	150	We missed the interment.
	151	A small long barrow.
	152 153 154	} Had been opened,
	155	This tumulus repaid us for the deficiency of the last seven. It is a fine bell-shaped barrow, 92 feet in diameter, and 11 in elevation. On the floor we found a large quantity of burnt bones, and with them an earthen cup of a singular and novel pattern, a cone of gold, five other articles of the same metal, and several curious ornaments of amber. The cup was unfortunately mutilated on one side, but its size and pattern are engraved in plate xxv. as well as the cone of gold, and the other articles, viz. a hornlike ornament of gold, two circular trinkets, composed of red amber, set round with gold, and several others, most of which had perforations in them, probably for suspension as ornaments for dress. We have opened as yet no barrow that produced such a

Page	No.	
201	155	variety of singular and elegant articles, both in pattern and design.

202 156 A fine bell-shaped barrow, contained within a very shallow cist, the remains of a skeleton, whose head was placed towards the west, with a deposit of various little elegant trinkets, engraved in plate xxv.; we also found another little grape cup, in high preservation. There was also a drinking cup at the feet of the skeleton.

157 Had a prior opening.

158 Though Dr. Stukelely has given an engraving of this barrow, under the title of BUSH BARROW, it does not appear that he ever attempted to open it. It was formerly fenced round, and planted with trees, and its exterior still bears a very rough appearance. The first attempts made by Mr. Cunnington in this barrow, proved unsuccessful, as did those of some farmers who dug into it; but in 1808 our researches were renewed, and we were amply repaid for our perseverance and former disappointment. On reaching the floor of the barrow, we discovered the skeleton of a tall and stout man, lying from south to north; the extreme length of his thigh bone was 20 inches; about 18 inches south of the head, were several brass rivets intermixed with wood, and some thin bits of brass nearly decomposed; near the shoulders lay the fine

Page	No.
202	158

brass celt engraved in plate xxvi which had been inserted in a handle of wood ; near the right arm was a large dagger of brass, and a spear head of the same metal, full 13 inches long, and the largest we had ever found. These were accompanied by a curious article in gold, which I conceive had originally decorated the case of a dagger. The handle of the spear or dagger exceeds any thing I have ever seen in execution, and can only be justly estimated by the engraving of it, in plate xxvii. We recognize in it the favorite zigzag ornament of the Britons, so prevalent in their urns, &c. Beneath the fingers of the right hand, lay a lance-head of brass, and immediately over the breast of the skeleton, was a large plate of gold, in the form of a lozenge, measuring 7 inches by 6, and decorated also by the zigzag ornament. It was fixed to a thin piece of wood, over the edges of which the thin pure gold was lapped, and being perforated at top and bottom, it is evident that it was intended for suspension, and probably over the breast in which situation it was found. On the right side of the skeleton was a curious perforated stone, some wrought articles of bone, many small rings of the same material, and another small article of gold, in in the form also of a lozenge. This

Page	No.
202	158

tumulus, the most interesting in its contents of any we have found, may be considered as the deposit of the chieftain of the clan.

| 205 | 159 160 |

Druid barrows; the former had been opened by Lord Pembroke or Dr. Stukeley; the latter produced within a small cist, an interment of burnt bones, with a great variety of amber, glass, and jet beads.

161 A skeleton with its head placed towards the south-east, accompanied by a drinking cup. Eighteen inches lower down was another lying on its left side, with its head towards the east; and beneath it we found a cist nearly six feet deep, cut in the chalk, and containing the primary interment of a young man, with his head lying towards the north, and a drinking cup, neatly ornamented close to his right hand.

Note.—In this barrow, we found the deposits of three skeletons, and by the position of the head of the third, we may conclude that the most ancient custom was that of placing the head to the north.

162 A fine Druid barrow which had a prior opening.

163 Burned bones, fragments of a small cup, and a pin of bone.

164 May be considered as the most beautiful

Page	No,	
205	164	bell-shaped barrow in the plains of Stonehenge. It contained within a very shallow cist, the skeleton of a man with his head placed to the north-east, upon a plank of elm wood; on the left side of his head, was a fine brazen dagger, and a small lance-head of the same metal, the former of which had been guarded by a case of wood; at the feet of the skeleton, was a richly ornamented drinking cup, there were also stag's horns at the head and feet.
206	165	A small oblong barrow, in which we found interments, as usual at the broad end.
	166	Contained the remains of a skeleton, with a drinking cup and stag's horns.
	167	A pond barrow.
	168	An interment of burnt bones.
	169	Did not prove sepulchral.
	170	A long barrow, not attempted, as in tumuli of this description, we have never found any thing to recompence our labours.
	171	A group of various tumuli, of different sizes, the largest of which produced a rude urn; nearly all the smaller ones contained simple interments of burnt bones.
	172	Contained burnt bones, black ashes, a

Page	No.
206	172

large ring, and several beads of a dark brown olive colour.

173 A long barrow. We never opened similar tumuli with any hopes of success, at eighteen inches from the surface, we found a skeleton, and on reaching the floor, four others strangely huddled together. One of the persons here interred, seems to have had no forehead, the sockets of his eyes appearing on the top of his head.

174 Had a prior opening.

175 A simple deposit of burnt bones.

176 A fine bell-shaped barrow, in which was a skeleton with its head towards the north, but the severity of the weather prevented our investigating this mound as minutely as we could have wished.

177 A deposit of burnt bones, with a fine spear-head of brass.

207 178 A simple interment of burnt bones.

179
180 } Had been opened by farmers.

181 A group of very mean barrows, which we did not think worthy of investigation as several showed marks of a prior opening.

182 Produced a deposit of burnt bones, that had been placed in a wooden box, and

Page	No.	
207	182	with them a brass dagger, which had been secured by a sheath of wood lined with linen cloth, a small lance-head, a pair of ivory nippers, and an ivory pin.
	183	Stag's horns, and burnt bones.

Pursuing from hence, a southerly direction, and crossing a little valley to the opposite hill, crowned with numerous tumuli, we come to a solitary barrow, composed entirely of flints, and although we discovered the cist, yet we perceived no signs of interment, or marks of a prior opening.

——✕₀✦₀✕——

WILSFORD GROUP OF BARROWS.

These are not numbered in the general plan, around Stonehenge, but on a separate sheet.—They consist of eighteen in number.

1 This barrow had been explored.

2 A very fine Druid barrow, which also had been opened, but not minutely examined, for on one side of the cist we found a neat lance-head of brass, and a pin of the same metal, intermixed with burnt bones.

3 Produced an interment of burnt bones by cremation, a considerable quantity of glass, amber, and jet beads, with a fine brass pin.

44

Page	No.	
207	4	In this barrow we missed the interment, finding only the cinerarium containing ashes,
208	5	Produced on the floor a simple interment of burnt bones, placed by the side of a circular cist, which contained another deposit of burnt bones, within a beautiful sepulchral urn, engraved in plate xxviii. Close to this urn was another cist, containing a singular deposit, with a spear-head of brass, which had been almost melted into a lump by the heat of the funeral pile.
	6	A Druid barrow whieh had been opened.
	7	Another Druid barrow, with three mounds within its area, in one of which we found the relics of the skeleton of a youth, and fragments of a drinking cup; in the central one was an interment of burnt bones, with a small brass pin, and the third appeared to have been opened.
	8	Had also been examined.
	9	This barrow produced within a cist, a little pile of burnt bones, with an ivory pin, a rude ring of bone, and a small brass celt, engraved in plate xxviii. The cist was protected by a thick covering of flints, and immediately over it was the skeleton of a dog.
	10	A pond barrow.

Page	No.	
208	11	Adjoining each other, the first had been
	12	opened and the scattered relics seem to indicate two interments, cremation, and a skeleton. The latter proved a singular though not a productive barrow, and required a good deal of skill and perseverance in opening; for we were obliged to dig ten feet below the level of the floor, before we came to the deposit of a skeleton, which was not accompanied by any arms or trinkets. We considered this as a very early British interment.
	13	Produced the skeleton of a young and very stout man, with the head towards the south-east, and near it a large and rude drinking cup, engraved in plate xxviii.
	14	A Druid barrow, which had experienced a prior opening.
209	15	We could find no interment.
	16	Produced a deposit of burnt bones, some instruments made of stag's horns, some whetstones, an arrow-head of flint, another in an unfinished state, and a small spear-head; at a greater depth was the primary interment of a skeleton with its head towards the north-west.
	17	Had been opened.
	18	This large bell-shaped barrow, may be considered as the monarch of this

group, both as to its superior size, as well as contents. On the floor we found the skeleton of a tall man, lying on his right side, with his head towards the south-east; at his feet were laid a massive hammer of stone, a brass celt, a tube of bone, and a handle for some instrument, a whetstone with a groove* in the centre, and several articles of bone, amongst which was the enormous tusk of a wild boar; but the most curious article was one of twisted brass, the use of which I cannot ascertain, it was unlike any thing we have yet found, and was evidently affixed to a handle. These articles are engraved in plate xxix.

LAKE GROUP OF BARROWS.

These barrows are also numbered on a separate plan.

1 | A long barrow.

2 | This diminutive tumulus, produced just under the surface, a very rude and perfect little cup, perforated at the bottom

---

* We have found numerons bits of bone, pointed at one end like a skewer, the use of which is exemplified by this stone with a groove, for on placing one of them in it, I found them fit exactly, and thus we know how the Britons sharpened their rude instruments of bone, with which they indented the decorations of their urns.

Page	No.	
209	2	like a cullender, with holes on the sides for suspension. It is engraved in plate xxx, and accompanied with an interment of burnt bones.
	3 4	} Had been previously opened.
	5	Contained burnt bones, with several small black beads.
	6	Is one of the finest barrows in this group, in which was a large sepulchral urn near the surface, placed with its mouth downwards, over a pile of burnt bones, amongst which was a fine ivory bodkin, engraved in plate xxx. At the further depth of five feet, were the remains of two skeletons, and at the total depth of thirteen feet nine inches, was the skeleton of a child, deposited in a cist with a drinking cup.
210	7	A large bell-shaped barrow, contained in a cist, a little pile of burnt bones, a very fine brass pin, a large bead of stone, another of ivory, and a lance-head of brass, engraved in plate xxx.
	8	A wide and flat barrow elevated about six feet from the ground, and supposed to be the one from which the French Prophets in the year 1710, delivered their doctrines to the multitude. Dr. Stukeley says "that the country people call this group the Prophet's barrows, because the French Prophets

Page	No.	
210	8	set up a standard on the largest barrow and preached to the enthusiastic multitude."

set up a standard on the largest barrow and preached to the enthusiastic multitude."

After making a very large section, we found on the north side a cist, eight feet and half long, and two feet wide, containing a pile of burnt bones, which had been enclosed within a box of wood, and near it a fine spear-head of brass, and a whetstone, engraved in plate xxviii.

9 — A simple interment of burnt bones.

211 — 10 — We made two trials in this barrow, but without success, having found nothing in it but the skeleton of a dog, and the head of a deer.

11
12 — Two fine Druid barrows, which, from the little trouble, had excited the curiosity of former antiquaries.

13 — Produced a simple interment of burnt bones.

14
15 — In these we see a kind of double barrow, the smallest end of which had been opened. The floor of the larger mound, was strewed with an immense quantity of wood ashes, in a small oblong cist, we found an interment of burnt bones, with four pretty glass beads, one of stone, two of amber, and a brass pin. This last barrow, is separated from the former group by the banks of an old enclosure. On the south side of it, are

Page	No.	
211	14	a few small tumuli, scarcely elevated
	15	above the surface, which were more productive than we had reason to expect.

	16	These five barrows claim a separate
	17	owner, and were carefully investigated
	18	by the Rev. Edward Duke, of Lake
	19	House, and their contents preserved by
	20	him. Each of the three first contained an interment of burnt bones, a small lance-head, but though No. 20 had also a lance-head, the uniformity was broken by four little curious articles of bone intermixed with the ashes. They are a novelty, and had their meaning and use in olden times; but I am at a loss to conjecture what their usage might have been; each of them has a separate mark on the surface, and they have been engraved in plate xxxi. Query— Might they have been used as *tesseræ*, or for casting lots, or some game? To the north of these are four other barrows.

| | 21 | Is a wide and low tumulus, and has been ploughed over for many years; it proved very rich in trinkets, &c., the more remarkable of which was a large ornament, composed of pieces strung together, and similar to the one engraved in plate iii, but larger in its dimensions. Besides the above, there were numerous beads of amber, larger than usual, and varying in their patterns, four articles of gold, perforated, and two small earthen cups. These ornaments are engraved of their full size in plate xxxi. |

Page	No.	
211	22	Had been partially opened, but amongst the burnt bones, we found fragments of two neatly ornamented drinking cups, and on further digging, we discovered the skeleton of a child, and over it a drinking cup, engraved in plate xviii.
	23	A simple interment of burnt bones.
	24	A similar interment with fragments of a drinking cup; immediately under the surface, and two feet lower down, was a deposit of burnt bones over the head of a skeleton; and beneath this, was a second skeleton lying with its head towards the north-west, and several pieces of stag's horns by its side.

Note.—The Numerals refer to the pages in my History of Ancient Wilts; and the Urns and other articles here described, are open to Public Inspection, in my Wiltshire Museum, at Stourhead.

J. Rutter, Printer, Shaftesbury.

PLATE I.

N.º 1. Long barrow.

Twin barrows.

4. Druid barrow.

PLATE II.

2. Bowl barrow.

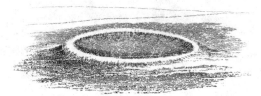

5. Pond barrow.

3. Bell barrow.

PLATE I.

Sepulchral Urn.

PLATE II.

Sepulchral Urn.

PLATE III.

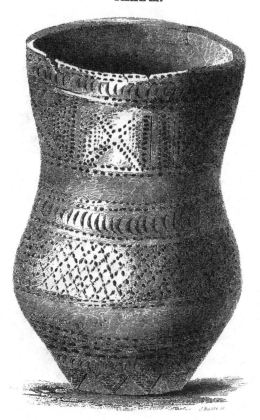

Drinking Cup.

PLATE IV.

Incense Cups.